BEDTIME BATTLES NO MORE!

Get Your Child to Sleep Through the Night in 10 Simple Steps

by
Emily Duffell

Bedtime Battles: No More

ISBN: 0-646-96465-8

ISBN-13: 978-0-646-96465-2

Disclaimer

First Edition

Table Of Contents

Preface

Thanks for purchasing my book. I have a story to tell and a lot of valuable information to share. If you are a parent of a growing baby, infant or energetic toddler, or perhaps you're an expectant mother eagerly anticipating a new addition to your family unit, then I think you will find this book a worthwhile resource.

Over the course of the book I shall endeavour to provide a valuable insight into the often challenging world of toddler sleep habits. Your young child's quality of sleep can have an impact on daytime performance, ongoing learning, development, adult sleep deprivation and your ability to function as a loving and devoted parent.

If you're already navigating ongoing issues settling your infant or toddler, your child is suffering frequent broken sleep, or you're beginning to question how much longer you can maintain a daily routine in absence of quality rest, then this book is designed to help. During the course of the book I will discuss why sleep is so important. This will include recommendations on the volume of sleep your toddler requires every day to optimise emotional control. I'll also provide a brief overview of the five stages of sleep, emphasising how each stage is critical to the development of your child.

I'll discuss a few of the commonly held myths of toddler and infant sleep, and try to understand a few excuses we as parents often make for our children's poor sleeping behaviour.

Time will be spent examining why it's so difficult to get your boy or girl to drift off to sleep and in particular I'll look at how sleep props and associations you are creating, perhaps unknowingly, impact your toddler's ability to fall asleep. You might be surprised by the influence a few of these are having on your night time routine and how you could be making a rod for your own back at bedtime.

I will refer to a variety of different sleep strategies promoted by sleep 'experts' in chapter five as well as touch on the importance of teaching your child to self-settle at bedtime, and throughout the evening.

Finally, I'll explore what actually works as well as what steps you should take to encourage your loveable but sometimes intolerable toddler to sleep. I will elaborate on what has and hasn't worked for me when endeavouring to provide my two much loved children the shuteye they (and I) require.

But, before I go into detail on the significance of sleep, I firstly want to impart a bit of background about me. Who am I and how am I equipped to talk to you about toddler sleeping habits?

I really hope you enjoy this book and that in some way it helps to alleviate the sleep issues you are experiencing with your toddler as well as enabling you to personally achieve a healthy and productive sleep routine.

Happy reading!

Emily

Chapter 1
My Story

Sleep is an immensely important and intensely personal endeavour. Issues that affect sleep patterns, and in turn individual health, can be miserable and down-heartening. I probably understand these impacts as adeptly as anyone.

Before I dive into the important and often debated topic of toddler sleep habits, and in advance of scrutiny of popular techniques to overcome the trials and tribulations of sleep, I thought it was important to provide some background on me, my experience, my family situation and why I believe I am suitably qualified to engage with you on this topic. How did I become a self-professed expert in the area of toddler sleep deprivation? Let's begin with my story.

Two Beautiful Girls

I am 34 years of age and a mother of two beautiful girls aged 7 and 3 with a very supportive husband who has always been a 'hands on' dad. Having kids is an absolute blessing. For countless years I had anticipated fondly the extension of my family unit and welcoming children into the world.

Our kids are and have always been the number one priority in both my husband and my lives. We love them dearly and have aspired to be dedicated, adoring and successful

1

parents; raising healthy, happy children that become an asset to society.

From the outset we've attempted to prioritise quality time with our family, engaging heavily in playtime, sleep time, reading, exploration, even creating unique little rituals for mundane daily activities. We've developed a unique bond with our children and (I hope) they appreciate our unfailing dedication and availability. I am sure most aspiring parents enjoy a similar connection.

Where possible my husband and I have undertaken to educate ourselves on key developmental milestones for our children. It always seemed a little difficult to maintain pace with the wealth of academic and parental advice although we (perhaps naively) believed we had a reasonable grasp on the sleeping habits of babies and toddlers.

This is where the 'but' moment comes in....

Preparing for a Lack of Sleep

Despite dedicating practically every thought and the majority of waking hours to manufacturing a smooth, successful child rearing experience... it became evident that life doesn't always mimic one's best laid plans. In preparing for a lack of sleep, a few years ago I stumbled across the expression that having a child is like 'having one foot in heaven and one foot in hell at the same time'. This utterance resonated with me at the time. I imagine that's why I still recall it. Needless to say it is no coincidence there is a four year gap between my two children.

My first child Amber was born in 2009. I loved my baby more than I felt anyone could ever understand. However, from the outset Amber was a terrible sleeper and I found myself overwhelmed by lack of sleep and my baby's recurrent needs throughout day and night.

Bedtime Battles: No More!

Don't get me wrong, I went into motherhood with eyes wide open. I expected to operate on limited sleep for a substantial period. I had read numerous books on child rearing to educate myself on the journey. A number of my close friends are at a similar life stage and we had discussed at length sleeping behaviours and strategies to manage acute sleep deprivation whilst effectively attending to the needs of our growing children.

I understood it was perfectly normal to function for weeks or even months on little more than three to four hours of unbroken sleep. Sleep deprivation is part of being a parent and any mum with young children knows this all too well.

Even the most contented child can inflict challenging periods where he or she wakes continually throughout the night. Many parents put temporary sleeping woes down to a period of poor health, teething or simply falling out of routine. Whatever the explanation, typically we as mothers endure the wrath as we attempt to be responsive and sensitive to our child's ever changing needs.

As strange as this may sound, in the early stages of parenthood I actually enjoyed being 'on call' and available to my baby at all hours, fulfilling nutrition and comforting needs as they arose. I would definitely wake in a bit of a bleary eyed fog but this seemed like a worthwhile side effect of attending to my growing baby. A coffee or two to kick start me in the morning always seemed to help.

I thought I had prepared myself for the only downside of motherhood, operating in a slightly sleep deprived state minus my customary eight hours. Nothing could have prepared me for this... as it turns out nothing could have prepared my husband and I for what was in store.

Nothing Could Have Prepared Us for This...

As a baby Amber was exceedingly difficult to settle. I'm not exaggerating when I say it would consistently take up to two hours to get her to sleep. After what seemed a marathon effort every time we tried to settle her, she would sleep for an unbelievably short period of time only to wake again. This was our routine for months and months. It was unbearable.

It didn't seem to matter whether it was day or night, getting her to sleep was a painstaking and emotionally draining experience. At night I would feed her every 3-4 hours only to spend the next 1-2 hours trying to coax her back to sleep.

I had a little understanding of the benefits of sleep and the critical role it played in my baby's learning, growth and development. I also had a little knowledge of how a developing brain is particularly vulnerable to sleep loss. Even though I had only a basic understanding of sleep advantages at that point, this heightened my anxiety at being unable to settle her into a deep sleep.

As any parent would want, I wanted my baby to engage in the world in a positive way. What became increasingly apparent to me was the impact of missed sleep on her behaviour. I know all parents have witnessed first hand the impact of a missed nap, delayed bedtime or interrupted sleep. Encountering sleep related behavioural problems on a near daily basis became particularly confronting.

Impact on Me as a Mother

Parents and babies both need sleep. Our bedtime struggles and frequent night wakings meant that neither Amber nor I were getting the sleep we required and it affected both of our moods appreciably. Not only that, chronic sleep deprivation was having a pronounced impact on my wellbeing.

As a parent I don't need to tell you that it's not easy caring for your baby, not to mention the rest of your family, if you are suffering from sleep deprivation.

I found it really challenging staying alert and maintaining focus on common daily tasks. I felt so tired I could barely remember my own name, let alone some of the important things I would normally be doing throughout the day. All of the normal daily chores like cleaning, cooking and washing were taking a back seat and causing a lot of unease in my mind.

My stress and anxiety levels seemed to be continually elevated in response to Amber's poor sleeping habits, the task of getting her to sleep and the lack of quality sleep I was receiving.

Enduring our arduous sleep settling routine for months on end was completely and utterly exhausting. I'm sure you're all aware of the fact that if babies don't sleep, neither do their parents; certainly not the mothers anyway.

I had friends who bragged about their children sleeping through the night at just 8 weeks of age. Instead of being happy for them, this was particularly deflating in my emotional state. Knowing that some parents were seemingly having a dream run of sleep with their newborns only compounded the anxiety I was experiencing.

All of these issues were affecting my attitude towards my role as a mother.

Impact on Family and Friends

Sleep deprivation is often considered an individual problem but it is actually a much broader health issue. Inadequate sleep affects our ability to function and impacts almost every social interaction with children, partners or spouses, friends and work colleagues.

I really felt the impact no sleep was having on my husband, family and friends. Being short of sleep was making me ill-tempered and intolerant. At the time I could sense myself being short, impatient or grumpy with others, something not normally in my nature, but I found it increasingly difficult to control my emotions. My poor husband would regularly bear the brunt of my sleep deprived state as I struggled to cope.

At times I felt I wasn't getting the emotional support I required. Time (and sleep) has improved my perspective. I now understand the difficulty others faced in trying to understand what I was going through and comprehending the appropriate avenues to provide support. I also realise that at the time I was probably struggling with my frame of reference.

The few times I managed to get some regular sleep provided some welcome relief. It also helped me feel like a more successful mother. The trouble was that periods of relief were few and far between.

I tried napping, which would occasionally help, although juggling the responsibilities of the household and my baby girl's constant needs made finding time to nap increasingly difficult. Close friends would advocate for me to ask for help when in need. While I appreciated the sentiment at the time, I didn't believe anyone other than me was in a position to effectively manage my situation or was really willing to endure an 'all-nighter' to care for my baby. Even if they were, the likelihood was she would have cried out for me anyway so I felt I was trapped in my sleep-deprived nightmare.

Trying to Convince Myself It Was Normal

My harrowing experience has taught me that a lot of mums underestimate the importance of achieving sufficient sleep. There are real risks of chronic sleep deprivation and the exhaustion that accompanies it. A few years ago when I became immersed in these issues I didn't take the impacts seriously enough. For a long long time I kept convincing myself it was a normal part of parenthood and I would soon reach the 'other side'.

A quick browse of the National Sleep Foundation of America's website illustrated to me that modern infants were sleeping less than the recommended 14-15 hours per day. This suggested others were enduring similar sleep issues and I should stick with it.

Unfortunately, my baby's irregular sleep patterns continued with seemingly no end.

I was never short of advice... everyone around me seemed to have some sort of advice they wished to share. Some of it was helpful, but much of it was not so beneficial. Friends would tell me to 'try this' and 'try that' or 'read this' and 'read that'. Others would suggest I savour this beautiful time with her. While I appreciated the ability to talk to friends about my experiences, I felt their well-meaning advice didn't really recognise the level of exhaustion and mental anguish I was going through.

Every morning I would get up wondering how I was going to cope with this routine all over again. Nothing we had tried seemed to work and I clung to the idea sleep deprivation was a normal part of parenting.

Diagnosed with Post Natal Depression

After months and months of feeling really low and coping with high levels of stress and anxiety, I became conscious this was more than the so called 'baby blues'.

Most mothers experience a few days or weeks of feeling emotional and overwhelmed, suffering mood swings, heightened anxiety, sadness or irritability. This can be associated with difficulty in sleeping. This experience is often termed the 'baby blues'.

I eventually realised my situation was more complicated. My inclinations were correct. I sought medical advice and was diagnosed as suffering post natal depression.

It seems it is common for post natal depression to be mistaken for baby blues in the first instance. The key difference between the two is the intensity and lasting nature of signs and symptoms associated with depression. The onset of depression can commonly occur during the early stage of child rearing, although the appearance of post natal symptoms can also surface beyond the first six months of child rearing.

Some of the more prevalent symptoms of post natal depression include:

• A diminished ability to concentrate, think clearly or make decisions

• Serious mood fluctuations

• Excessive tearfulness and crying

• Loss of appetite or overeating

• Intense irritability and anger

• Feelings of guilt or inadequacy

• Fearing you are not a good mother

• Difficulty bonding with your child

• Extreme fatigue or low energy

• Withdrawing from family and friends

• Reduced pleasure in activities you typically enjoy

• Anxiety and panic attacks

• Thoughts of self-harm

In some respects understanding I had a serious medical issue provided relief. It wasn't just an inability to cope with being a mother. I had a diagnosed condition that required attention and medication. On the flip side knowing I had a mental health issue accentuated the feelings of failure I was already experiencing.

A significant proportion of new mums suffer postnatal depression. According to the Centre for Disease Control an estimated 15% of women become depressed during the first year of their baby's life. Many suffer in silence, not recognising they require assistance or unaware of where to find it. In fact, some experts believe up to 50% of postnatal cases go unrecognised or untreated. Commonly mothers will dismiss the idea of depression due to the stigma associated with it.

Sleep deprivation does not only impact one's ability to raise children it can also place a mother at a significantly higher risk of developing post natal depression. This was a primary contributor for me.

An increasing body of research into infant sleep problems and maternal depression has identified a direct association between improving sleep and minimising symptoms of depression. A community based study by Hiscock and Wake in 2001 proposed appropriate anticipatory guidance addressing infant sleep to decrease maternal depressive symptoms.

Untreated, postnatal depression may worsen, or last for many months or longer. Recognising you have an issue is often the first hurdle to addressing depression symptoms.

We Tried Literally Everything to Get Our Baby to Sleep

As my husband and I continued through this difficult period with a lack of sleep, we did so with the knowledge that sleep deprivation was having a pronounced impact on my wellbeing. It became increasingly important for us to get our baby girl to settle.

We felt we had tried everything to get Amber into a regular sleeping pattern. And when I say everything, I really mean anything and everything.

Our inability to get Amber into a deep long lasting sleep had us constantly questioning our routine, techniques and the health of our child. Had we over stimulated our baby? Was I overestimating the amount of sleep my little girl needed? Perhaps things would settle down when she got onto solids? Did she have an underlying medical issue? Several visits to the doctor alleviated these concerns.

We had tried most of the more common methods including a lot of shhhhing (no doubt you too are an expert in the creation of light shhhhhing noises), rhythmic back patting or gentle rocking. We tried remaining in our baby's room until she was just drifting off to sleep before stealthily sneaking out. We engaged in short term co-sleeping, staying in her room until we thought she was safely in a deep sleep.

Nothing seemed to work.

'Crying it Out'

Many of our friends advocated the 'crying it out' method and letting the baby cry themself to sleep. We had several attempts at this much-publicised technique. The underlying theory is that allowing your baby to 'cry it out' and fall asleep on their own accord will break poor sleep associations. We would set limits as to when we would and wouldn't respond during nap times and in the evenings.

Unfortunately, our baby would cry progressively louder and longer to the point where her voice would become hoarse and we thought she would make herself physically ill. It was distressing not only for our baby but for us as well. I would often end up in tears. Crying it out just did not seem to be working. Subsequent attempts yielded similar results.

Sleep School

Sleep school operates on the premise that sleep is a habit and can therefore be learned. In Australia, sleep school is covered under the public health system following doctor referral but there are several private options also available. There is a range of options including an intensive two day visit through to a weeklong intervention. A sleep specialist oversees your unit and each family is assigned a specialist sleep nurse.

I understand that this approach works for some families experiencing sleep issues but not all. Unfortunately it didn't work for us at all, providing no improvements in our sleep routine.

Specialist Maternal Health Nurse

A specialist maternal health nurse began visiting us at home. This served as a good opportunity to articulate the issues we were having and the health nurse provided information and advice on managing sleep, alongside other general toddler challenges.

Sleep practitioners provide a more holistic approach to establishing healthy sleep habits. While it was useful to have a regular sounding board for issues, unfortunately the techniques proposed failed to improve our situation.

As you can imagine we were at the stage when we would try anything for a decent night's sleep. You will probably laugh at this... but we even recorded ourselves singing, and left this to play at our daughter's door to trick her into believing we were right outside!

Sadly but foreseeably, this didn't provide a marked difference in the sleep routine of Amber either... and needless to say it didn't help my sleep deprivation.

From Cot to Bed

By the time Amber was two and a half years of age she was ready to shift from a cot into a bed. She has always been a tall girl and still is, and there came the time when the cot was not big enough for her anymore. We had been shopping to pick out the cutest bed and allowed her to pick her own special doona cover. In the back of my mind I hoped she would be super excited about the new sleeping environment - and that might seduce her into an improved sleeping routine.

Tragically, moving to a bed was a new nightmare in itself. You guessed it. She would not stay in her bed. Instead of rolling over and falling into a deep slumber... she would get out of bed and make her way into the family room every two minutes to find me. And it didn't just happen once.... it occurred all evening long. The next day she would be very difficult because she was so exhausted.

Being put to bed, up again to roam the house, repeat, repeat, repeat! The cot was bad, but I was beginning to think the bed may be even worse!

Progress... Finally

After a few more long and arduous months of agony, I am happy (and relieved) to say that Amber did learn to stay in her bed and is now a fantastic sleeper. I really felt like this day would never come. The impact that my sleeping child has had on her and my state of mind has been remarkable. It has provided me with an entirely different perspective on things.

So what was it that worked in the end? Getting our toddler to sleep was not due to one single element. In the end it was a combination of things including persistence, routine and the addition of a sleep training clock. There is no one thing that will work for everyone and trial and error is often a big part of the process. However, if you have a baby or toddler that isn't sleeping it's time to change things up.

How I Got to Where I Am Today

Finally, we had overcome our toddler's sleeping issues. At this point, with a new outlook and increasing energy levels, we decided we were never ever going through that ordeal again. We desperately wanted to add to our small family of three, so simply avoiding the addition of another child wasn't an option. I needed to develop a better plan of attack.

My experience and the associated sleep deprivation for the initial three years of my child's life persuaded me of the need to learn as much as I could about toddler sleeping habits to circumvent a similar experience with my second child and maybe help other parents in a similar position to mine.

I buried myself in academic research, reviewed the latest information and emerging trends on improving toddler sleep patterns. And I am proud to say that it paid off.

Our second baby girl was born in 2013. Ellie is a fantastic sleeper and was great at sleeping from a young age. The techniques and structures we put in place from the outset have been extremely successful in creating an environment for her sleep patterns to flourish.

This was a massive relief for both my husband and I, and confirmed for us our new approach to sleep was an advantageous one. Off the back of this experience I now consult regularly on the impact of sleep to try to assist other mothers struggling with toddlers sleeping abnormalities.

One of the successful techniques we employed with our second child as she progressed into the toddler years was the adoption of a sleep training clock into her routine. This complimented our settling efforts extremely well and the clock was effective at teaching good sleeping habits. However, there were several features that this sleep training clock didn't possess that we knew would have been beneficial in streamlining and expediting the sleep adoption process. For this reason, we spent the next two years creating and inventing our own toddler sleep training clock to not only teach children when to go to bed and stay in bed but to help exhausted parents reclaim their sleep!

To those currently struggling with sleep, my heart goes out to you, because I have been there and I understand how tough this period in your life can be. Perhaps it is time to rethink your approach, to take a look at it with fresh eyes. I will attempt to help you with changing that perspective throughout the course of this book as I unearth greater detail on the critical area of children's sleep.

Firstly, I want to explore why sleep is so important for both toddler and parent.

Chapter 2
Why Is Sleep So Important?

Ok, you've now heard my narrative on the impact chronic sleep deprivation had on my family and I. Thankfully this period in our life is consigned to history and I possess two gorgeous children who (more often than not) sleep the entire night, providing my husband and I with a quality night's sleep and a substantially more positive outlook on life!

I am conscious my story is by no means unique. Sleeping complications are increasingly prevalent throughout modern society. Everyone experiences the pain, frustration or fatigue associated with broken sleep at some stage in their life, regardless of whether they are parent to a bustling toddler or expanding family.

Millions of people worldwide struggle with ongoing sleep problems or issues. In fact, recent research has indicated most of us require more sleep than we obtain on a nightly basis.

A National Health Interview Survey (USA) proclaimed approximately 30% of adults achieved fewer than six hours sleep a night in the years 2005-2007. More recently, a 2012 study chronicled a low 63% of 15 year olds nightly sleep fulfilling seven or more hours. This number was down from a reported 72% in 1991. Perhaps the most concerning revelation was youths who were failing to attain required sleep volumes still believed their sleep durations were adequate.

With sleep acting as a primary pillar of good health, placing emphasis on achieving recommended levels of restorative sleep is of utmost importance.

A multitude of theories exist as to why we may be getting less sleep. Dr David Schulman of the Emory Clinic Sleep Disorders Laboratory in Atlanta, Georgia believes modern day life has greater distractions and this could be reducing the importance individuals place on a good night's rest. Schulman cited the internet, smart devices, playing games and TV as common entertainment options interfering with routine sleep.

It seems round the clock access to work, technology, friends and family enables individuals to remain increasingly active late into the evening. The once common pastime of blissful relaxation, winding down from the day's events, is now considered a luxury. An unfortunate side effect of this increasingly connected life is an intensification in stress. It now feels difficult to escape deadlines, even in the comfort of one's own home. Heightened stress levels are associated with sleeplessness, anxiety and depression. Study into factors that affect sleep health is relatively immature; however it is a rapidly expanding area of research.

What Do We Know About Sleep?

One of the primary features of sleep is that it is an active and dynamic act. It's easy to consider sleep simply as a time when you switch off your brain to recharge for the following day. As it turns out the brain and body are extremely active at various points of the sleep cycle and this dynamic activity plays a particularly influential role in human performance while awake.

Considerable progress has been achieved in refining techniques to understand brain activity during sleeping hours. Neuroimaging procedures such as MRI, or functional magnetic resonance imaging, allow us to detect changing activity in parts of the brain through changes in blood flow. Through Positron Emission Tomography (PET) scientists map functional processes in the brain using small amounts of short lived radioactive material. Electroencephalography (EEG) measures 'brain waves' or electrical activity using electrodes strategically placed on a patient's scalp.

Most individuals understand a good night's sleep is beneficial to prepare for the challenges of a new day as well as the general role it plays in improving quality of life.

Despite this, the importance of sleep is not given the significance it requires. Let's take a look at why sleep is important, not only for your growing baby or toddler, but also for the adults heavily engaged in this critical child rearing process.

The Impact of Sleep on Healthy Brain Function

Sleep is a restorative function. It allows your body to repair itself physiologically and psychologically. This repair and rejuvenation process is central in maintaining healthy brain function.

Scientists in the January 2016 issue of Proceedings of the National Academy of Science suggest research data is consistent with "the idea that sleep is primarily devoted to the critical activities of repair and reorganisation in the brain, not the whole body, and that this reorganisation probably includes learning and memory". The academics hypothesised that other components of the body repair and restore themselves without the necessity for a sleeping state, rendering the function of sleep as primarily a restorative brain function.

(http://news.harvard.edu/gazette/story/2007/03/sleep-found-to-repair-and-reorganizethe-brain/)

While an interesting perspective, this is perhaps too simplistic a view. Other sources suggest sleep does play a critical role in the rejuvenation and development process throughout the body.

For example, according to scientists from the University of Wisconsin, quality sleep boosts the manufacture of cells (termed oligodendrocytes) responsible for forming Myelin.

What is Myelin? Myelin is located on nerve cells within the brain and spinal cord providing an insulation type function around nerve endings. Its primary role is to allow efficient movement of electrical nerve impulses throughout the body. Think of it as similar to the electrical wiring in your house... electrical currents move efficiently along said wiring, aided by insulation. Sleep boosts cognitive ability. Do you find yourself struggling to pay attention to your children, friends or perhaps work colleagues throughout the day? Is your toddler having difficulty with seemingly simple problem solving tasks or decision making? A lack of sleep could be to blame.

Sleep is a key determinant of how well you or your child thinks, reacts and interacts. Obtaining an appropriate volume of sleep will boost decision-making, motivation, productivity and your ability to retain or reproduce historical occurrences.

There are times when my children seem to have the proverbial attention span of a goldfish. I manage to gain their attention for a split second before they are distracted again searching for a new task to engage in.

Yes, kids are often impulsive and easily diverted. However, sleep increases a child's attention span. In fact, research has demonstrated children who consistently sleep more than ten hours per night up until the age of three experiences three times less hyperactivity, impulsivity and distractibility issues. Not only does sleep play an active role in short term cognitive performance, it has a profound impact on learning and development. The human brain encompasses a hugely complex network of nerve cells. For learning to occur a healthy toddler's brain is continually constructing new nerve pathways based on their experiences and interactions - forming the process for learning and developing new skills.

In fact, when your baby is born it already possesses all the neurons (or nerve cells) it will ever need. The key to learning is the configuration of an appropriate 'wiring pattern' to provide the necessary structure to enhance learning, perform movement, language or cognitive behaviours.

Scientists often discuss the importance of 'essential nourishment' in order for your child to nurture healthy brain development. The term 'nourishment' is a particularly broad reference in this case and can include experiences, nutrition, love and attention.

Nourishment also includes sleep. A key to healthy brain development and optimal learning is achieving appropriate levels of quality sleep. Sleep is integral to help us better understand the information we have absorbed.

A study published in the Journal of Neuroscience by researchers from Brown University positively associated sleep with the adoption of simple motor tasks. The experiment involved a series of simple finger tapping tasks performed with the non-dominant hand. Neural activity was assessed using magnetoencephalography (MEG) and sleep phase was tracked using polysomnography (PSG) and MRI.

The investigation compared one group, allowed to sleep for three hours, against another group who were required to remain awake. Interestingly, those that slept performed the simple motor task faster and more accurately than those deprived of sleep.

Two specific brainwave oscillations were identified in the top-middle part of brain in a supplementary motor area (SMA). The scientists hypothesised that this specific motor area played an important role in "reorganization" the brain carries out during sleep, in order to encourage motor learning.

There are many other studies demonstrating the significant impact sleep has on boosting learning performance of children, even babies only a few days old. One such study completed by researchers at Columbia University Medical Center demonstrated that children as young as 1-2 days old learn during their sleep.

How did they establish that? Well, the research team played specific sounds to sleeping newborns, and immediately afterwards administered a light puff of air on their eyelids. Following only twenty minutes of this intervention babies had learnt to anticipate the air puff, squinting immediately after the sound.

It seems it is not only nightly rest that contributes to learning. A baby or toddler's daily naps are recognised as playing a vital role. A group of 40 pre-schoolers were investigated by neuroscientists at the University of Massachusetts to review the impact of napping on learning and memory retention. Researchers compared performance in a memory style game when engaging in daily naps (on average 77 minutes per day), versus no sleeping during the day. Napping toddlers exhibited significantly improved memory retention up to 24 hours later. Children without naps failed to recall 15% of what they had learned whereas those who napped recalled 100% of memory tasks.

I am sure almost every parent yearns for their child to develop a creative imagination. Emerging studies have linked REM (Rapid Eye Movement) sleep with improved creativity. [Note: REM is one of the key stages of sleep. We'll touch on this in more detail in the following chapter so stay tuned!]

At the University of California researchers examined three groups of subjects; resting with no sleep; non REM sleep; and engaging in REM sleep. Using a protocol called the Remote Associates Test (RAT) scientists were able to quantify increases in creativity.

They established that subjects recently woken from REM sleep demonstrated improved creativity, whereas those in the alternative groups exhibited no change. The scientists suggested that REM sleep enhances creativity and plays a prominent role in formation of associative networks in the brain.

Are you feeling particularly grumpy or emotional? Did you wake up on the wrong side of the bed? While this is a popular catchphrase it is unlikely to be the cause of your foul mood! It's more likely you've been short changed a couple of hours of sleep.

Not only is adequate sleep consequential in healthy brain development, it plays a critical role in regulating your mood, controlling emotional responses and reducing stress.

Drift off into a deep sleep and the specific brain area associated with controlling emotions takes a well-earned break.

I am sure, like me, you know all too well the emotional impact a lack of sleep can have on a child, turning the most even tempered toddler into an emotional wreck impossible to reason with. But why is sleep so instrumental in keeping one's emotions in check?

A 2007 study in Current Biology from the University of California examined the association between sleep starved brains and emotional state. They identified a disconnection in the prefrontal cortex, the part of the brain responsible for keeping emotions in check, inhibiting the ability of subjects to maintain consistent emotions. The intervention compared 36 hour sleep starved individuals against a control group adhering to normal sleeping behaviour. The research team presented images of an increasingly disturbing nature to participants. The sleep deprived group were significantly more overwhelmed; demonstrating emotional centres 60% more active than the well slept control group.

If you find yourself feeling particularly emotional or perhaps flying off the handle when you are lacking sleep, just remember it's completely normal. Sleep deprivation can play havoc with our emotional compass. If researchers are demonstrating a 60% higher emotional response after a single night of sleep deprivation, then you can begin to comprehend how ongoing nights, weeks or even months of sleep shortage can leave you emotionally drained.

A Range of Physical Health Benefits

The physical health benefits of consistent, high calibre sleep are seemingly endless. Let's start by investigating the key role sleep plays in cell growth and repair. Growth hormone is an important peptide hormone secreted by the pituitary gland. The hormone plays a primary role in stimulating cell regeneration and reproduction. Deep sleep, a restorative and regenerative form of sleep, is associated with the release of growth hormone.

Bedtime Battles: No More!

Babies spend half their daily life in deep sleep and, according to Judith Ownes, Director of sleep medicine at the Children's National Medical Centre in Washington DC, growth hormone release plays a central role in the rapid growth of your bustling boy or girl. In fact, a, study into sleep characteristics in children with growth hormone deficiency by Verrillo et al found a decrease in total sleep time, sleep efficiency and stage 2 non REM sleep. This indicated that children with insufficient levels of growth hormone may sleep less deeply than children exhibiting healthy growth hormone profiles. When you complained of a specific ailment as a youngster did your mum always tell you all you needed was a good night's rest? Mine certainly did. At the time I remember it was easy to dismiss as the equivalent of an old wives' tale. But seemingly there is a strong link between sleep and effective functioning of your immune system.

A type of protein known as cytokines are produced by the body as you sleep. This protein plays a vital role in fighting illness, infection and stress. Lack of sleep can impact the availability of cytokines to combat germs.

A recent study at the Centre for Health and Community sought to understand the role lack of sleep plays in immunity. The researchers used a cold virus, selectively exposing unwitting subjects after a review of their sleep status.

Not surprisingly, individuals achieving more sleep were at lower risk of contracting the illness. Patients who achieved seven or more hours per night were four times less likely to become unwell than the group sleeping for six or fewer hours.

Not only does adequate sleep defend your body from short term ailments through superior immune function, it may also reduce the risk of chronic disease. Lower sleep is correlated with increased prevalence of high blood pressure, diabetes and heart disease.

This association may in part be behavioural. Quality sleep encourages more positive health behaviours such as improved nutritional practices and an increased likelihood of exercising, both actions that decrease the risk of heart related complaints. These positive health behaviours also have an advantageous impact on weight control.

Sleep inadequacy can effect impulse control. The frontal lobe in your brain plays an essential role in impulse management. A lack of sleep has been shown to limit its influence.

I'm sure you can associate with this yourself. When you are tired it's so easy to opt for a quick 'pick me up' - perhaps a large latte or high carb snack. It's also really appealing to skip planned exercise and choose convenient takeaway over a nutritious home cooked meal. Research backs this up. A study published in the American Journal of Clinical Nutrition in January 2009 established that sleep deprived subjects were more prone to late night snacking and selecting unhealthy high carbohydrates food choices. A good night's sleep will provide the mental clarity to make beneficial nutritional and health decisions.

Do you have aspirations for your toddler to become a sports star of note? The role of sleep in improving motor control, reducing injury risk, and promoting healing and repair should not be discounted.

A 2000 study by Williamson & Fever illustrated a single night without sleep can reduce reaction times by over 300%. Equally disturbing was that a good night's rest was insufficient to recover from sleep debt. Recovery after a poor night's sleep can take several days. The implications of this are much greater than just on the sports field.

Children are clumsier and more impulsive when sleep deprived, and (according to a study into Chinese school children receiving less than 9 hours per night) are more likely to endure injuries requiring medical intervention.

Another study completed by Milewski et al in 2014 supports this claim. Researchers analysed injury factors relating to high school athletes and hypothesised that hours slept was the biggest predictor of injury.

Normally mistakes are not particularly threatening and transpire in and around your home. But they can be. A lack of sleep can cause what is termed 'microsleep', brief moments of sleep that occurs while you are still awake. There are a number of scenarios where sleep deficiency can be particularly dangerous such as when driving. Drowsy drivers often believe it is not impairing their performance. The reality is stark. In fact according to the National Sleep Foundation's 2005 Sleep in America poll, 60% of drivers admit to driving drowsy, and 37% have fallen asleep at the wheel. That equates to 103 million people. It is likely the ratios are similar for other countries as well.

The US National Highway Traffic Safety Administration conservatively estimated that driver drowsiness was a factor in 100,000 car accidents reported to the police, including 1550 tragedies, over 70,000 injuries at a cost of over 10 billion dollars.

Sleep deficiency has also played a role in a number of high profile and tragic accidents. The Exxon Valdez oil spill crisis in 1989 could potentially have been averted but for third mate Gregory Cousins falling asleep at the helm. American Airways Flight 1420 overshot the runway in 1999 killing 11 and injuring hundreds. It was later determined impaired performance from fatigue was a contributing factor.

Ensuring a good night's rest preserves focus, maintains alertness, and reactiveness, playing a prominent role in the safety of not only yourself and your family but also others.

So What Happens When You Do Not Get Enough Sleep?

Ok, I have mentioned a few of the key benefits of avoiding sleep debt. Let's talk in a bit more detail about what happens when you don't get enough sleep. One of the key drawbacks of sleep deficiency, whether acute or chronic, is that a person's brain works harder... while accomplishing less.

At best a lack of sleep might lead to a lot of yawning, a slight lack of concentration, erratic memory, short lasting irritability or grumpiness and minimal impact on general coordination. But the aftermath of sleep deprivation can be far more damaging.

Sleep deprivation is generally categorised as acute or chronic. Acute sleep deprivation refers to a lack of or reduction in sleep time typically lasting up to one or two days, at which point the sleep debt is 'caught up'. The host of short term repercussions are generally alleviated soon after sleep patterns return to normal. Then there is chronic sleep deprivation; long lasting sleep inadequacy where a person habitually sleeps for less than the amount needed for optimal health and performance.

It pays to note, lack of sleep quantity is not necessarily the primary cause of this. It is feasible to be sleep deprived when achieving recommended total volumes of sleep. A frequent example of this is when operating outside of a normal sleep and waking routine, such as during shift work, or when sleep is regularly broken owing to external influences. Yes, such as constant waking from your new baby or toddler!

For the purpose of this book I intend to focus predominantly on chronic sleep deprivation and the ongoing impact this can have on the family unit - including toddlers and Mum or Dad.

First, what causes this chronic sleep deprivation in toddlers or parents? The answers may seem quite obvious, but for the sake of clarity, insufficient sleep can be the outcome of a range of causative factors. It may be that like me, baby or family needs are impacting upon your sleep structure. Or, your work demands may have increased. Or, you may be suffering from a sleep disorder or medical complication.

We'll touch on the multitude of sleep disorders in a little more detail later in this chapter, but first I'd like to explore some of the very real risks of chronic sleep deprivation.

Risks of Chronic Sleep Deprivation

I have already discussed the benefits of a good night's sleep to healthy brain function and general physical or emotional health. Of course the opposite is true with a prolonged lack of quality sleep.

Inadequate sleep can interfere with or alter activity in particular parts of your brain. At its extreme this can have serious consequences. Let's examine a few of the daunting implications of persistent sleep deprivation.

Fact: Sleep deprivation affects the ability to learn.

A number of studies citing that children with a lack of sleep demonstrate lower grades, particularly in subjects such as maths, reading and writing.

Fred Danner, a professor at the University of Kentucky, completed a study investigating sleeping habits and its impact on school grades on 882 high school freshmen. His 2008 research positively associated hours of sleep per school night with GPA (grade point average) as well as significantly impacting level of motivation. He also demonstrated lower incidence of clinically significant levels of emotional disturbance for students achieving higher nightly sleep.

(http://www.aasmnet.org/articles.aspx?id=873)

Fact: Sleep deprivation can lead to behavioural problems.

I don't think this fact will come as any surprise to parents of toddlers or preschool children.

We've probably all been exposed to cranky, tearful, tantrum wielding children following a night or two of substandard sleep, at least on occasion.

But these behavioural problems are short lived right? Maybe. The University College London's Epidemiology & Public Health Department investigated the effect of irregular bedtimes on behavioural problems. The study, published in the journal Paediatrics, analysed data from 10,000 children in the United Kingdom aged 3, 5 and 7 years of age.

(http://www.medicalnewstoday.com/articles/267366.php)

The bad news for parents who struggle to maintain a consistent bedtime was that there was a clear link between bedtimes and behaviour. They established that irregular sleep timing caused deprivation, disruption to natural body rhythms, could compromise brain maturation and had a marked impact on behaviour.

Behaviour analysis included a review of hyperactivity, conduct problems, issues maintaining emotions and social interaction difficulties. There was a worsening of scores as subjects progressed throughout childhood without a consistent and appropriate bedtime.

Professor Yvonne Kelly, the lead researcher, suggested that "not having fixed bedtimes, accompanied by a constant sense of flux, induces a state of body and mind akin to jet lag and this matter for healthy development and daily functioning."

The upside of this research was the revelation that interventions creating a regular night-time routine provided obvious improvements in behaviour.

Fact: Sleep deprivation can severely impact emotional health.

I talked about the considerable impact sleep difficulties had on my psychological health earlier.

A key driver is an increase in the level of the stress hormone cortisol. Elevated cortisol levels can radically impact behaviour and mood, not only for your child (cue temper tantrums!) but also for you as a parent. I found myself disciplining my daughter in situations or for behaviours that probably wouldn't have fazed me in the slightest had I been functioning in a well-rested and emotionally stable state.

All of a sudden my toddler's quirky habits or nuances, ordinarily borderline endearing in nature, I found irritable, often driving angry or impulsive responses. The driver was an elevation in cortisol levels.

After a loss of sleep, the profile of Cortisol levels is altered, resulting in an elevation of cortisol levels the next evening. A study published in Sleep back in 1997 investigated the impact of acute partial or total sleep deprivation on the night-time and daytime profile of cortisol. The researchers established that sleep loss could modify the resiliency of an individual's stress response, accelerating cognitive and metabolic consequences of glucocorticoid excess.

(http://www.ncbi.nlm.nih.gov/pubmed/9415946)

An ongoing lack of sleep can be much more impactful than simply administering short term tension, vigilance or irritability. Chronic sleep inadequacy can contribute to more severe mood related symptoms.

Enduring a period where you feel sad or low is not unusual. Everyone experiences ups and downs in daily life. However, persistent feelings of sadness, anxiety, disinterest or hopelessness are symptoms of depression, a far more serious mental and emotional health issue. The symptoms of depression can't simply be ignored. In most cases they won't just go away. Depression is a serious disorder that requires attention.

A complex relationship exists between depression and sleep. For some individuals depression leads to sleep problems such as insomnia. For others sleep deprivation can play an integral role in contributing to mental health disorders, such as was the case with my post natal depression diagnosis. It is estimated that three quarters of patients with depression experience some kind of sleeping disorder.

Generalised anxiety disorder is another emotional health complaint influenced by chronic sleep inadequacy. Experts believe sleep issues strengthen the risk of developing anxiety. Certainly a large proportion of individuals experiencing anxiety disorders are affected by sleep problems, estimated at over 50%. Young children suffering from anxiety sleep less deeply and typically require longer settling times than children unaffected by this complaint.

Psychiatric problems such as attention deficit hyperactivity disorder (ADHD) can be accentuated in children with sleeping problems. Even when a child does not meet the diagnostic criteria for ADHD, sleeping issues drive hyperactive and inattentive behaviour. Promisingly, a 2006 study suggested treating sleep problems may be sufficient to eradicate attention and hyperactivity for some children.

(http://www.ncbi.nlm.nih.gov/pubmed/17118097?dopt=Abstr actPlus)

Fact: Sleep deprivation increases the risk of serious health issues.

There are seemingly endless lists of health complaints sleep issues can contribute or predispose individuals to. The least impactful include headaches, aching muscles and periorbital puffiness. Periorbital puffiness sounds serious, but don't worry, this is just the commonly known "bags under eyes". Not great for complexion but otherwise relatively harmless.

There are however, a range of serious complaints you could be susceptible to if you suffer from chronic sleep deprivation.

These risks include:

• **Increased chance of heart disease including stroke, heart attack or high blood pressure.** Sleep is critical for healthy heart function. Regardless of age, weight, physical health or smoking habits, a lack of sleep increases risk of cardiovascular disease. One study concluded that sleeping fewer than six hours per night rendered you twice as susceptible to the threat of stroke or heart attack as those who sleep six to eight hours an evening.

• **Heightened Diabetes Type 2 risk and impairments in glucose metabolism.** Sleep loss can affect glucose metabolism, increase insulin levels and elevate the risk of diabetes.

• It is believed a lack of sleep may lead to higher likelihood of kidney disease. Scientists from Brigham and Women's Hospital in Boston found women who slept five hours or less per night experienced a rapid decline in kidney function compared to women achieving a healthier seven to eight hours per night.

(http://www.webmd.com/sleepdisorders/news/20151105/poor-sleep-might-harm-kidneys-study-suggest)

• **Tissue damaging inflammation.** Sleep loss can play a key role in triggering the cellular pathway that causes inflammation and fights against healthy organs and tissues.

• **Severe skin complaints.** A lack of sleep can inflict significant lesions or damage on skin ranging from eczema, psoriasis to atopic dermatitis. It can also increase the impact of ageing.

• **Increased risk of Fibromyalgia.** Fibromyalgia is a condition associated with widespread musculoskeletal pain, and associated with fatigue, memory and mood issues. The likelihood of succumbing to this nasty pain disorder is increased for individuals with sleep problems according to a 2011 examination.

Fact: Lack of sleep may cause you or your child to become overweight.

Yes, failure to get the required amount of sleep could hit you right around the waistline. It may sound a little fanciful, but there is increasing evidence sleep loss causes kids to become overweight or even obese. What's more, some experts believe impacts begin during infant years.

Children who are sleep deprived often have divergent eating patterns compared to well-rested kids. They tend to crave high fat or higher carb foods when drowsy or overtired. What's more, sleep deprivation impacts the behaviour of two hormones, Ghrelin and Leptin, integral to advising our brain when we are satiated. Modifying the influence of these hormones can increase appetite, encourage overeating and weight gain.

Sleep deprivation can also compromise a child's motivation to participate in active tasks, resulting in lower daily energy expenditure and calorie burning. OK, I have talked a fair amount about the important of sleep and the substantial impacts sleep deficiency can have on human performance. Hopefully this has given you an insight into the importance of getting sufficient rest both personally and for your growing toddler.

If there is one positive to take out of the consequences of inadequate sleep it is that in many instances a lack of sleep is caused by behavioural factors and these can most often be managed by making sleep a priority and establishing a superior routine. Even for the worst sleeping toddler, sleeping is a habit that can be learned. I worked this out the hard way the first time round… but we'll get onto how in a bit more detail soon.

However, in some instances a lack of sleep is not necessarily a behavioural issue that can be easily remedied. Occasionally a sleep disorder is central to you or your child's inability to obtain the appropriate amount of sleep. In fact statistics from the National Commission on Sleep Disorders Research in America estimate 10-15% (at least 40 million) people encounter ongoing sleep disorders with a further 20-30% suffering intermittent issues.

Common / Contributing Sleep Disorders (In Children and Adults)

Sometimes it's not a failure to take yourself off to bed at an appropriate time, or continued interruption from kids driving sleep deprivation issues. A range of distinct sleep disorders exist with contrasting levels of seriousness.

While each disorder is in some way distinct, the majority possess one of the following characteristics; difficulty commencing or maintaining sleep; excessive daytime sleepiness; or experiencing abnormal sensations, movements or behaviours during ones sleep.

I am going to touch on a few of these sleep afflictions with some details of each disorder to consider whether your toddler's or personal sleeping issues warrant further investigation.

Before doing that however, I want to reiterate what I said above. The majority of children's sleeping problems stem from environmental or behavioural influences. It's really easy to jump off the deep end; convinced that a medical condition underlies your loved one's sleep fluctuations when most often this is not the case.

The categorisation of sleep disorders are slightly different depending on which research or sleep society you subscribe to. For the purpose of our discussion we'll distinguish six categories of sleep disorders as published in ICSD-3 (The International Classification of Sleep Disorders). This classification lists Insomnias, Sleep Related Breathing Disorders, Hypersomnolence: Central Disorders, Circadian Rhythm Sleep-Wake Disorders, Parasomnias and Sleep-Related Movement Disorders.

Insomnia

You have probably heard the term insomnia bandied about, but what is it? Insomnia refers to a short lived or long term disruption to the sleep cycle. It can last a few days or several weeks and months.

Insomnia is typically categorised by problems dropping off or remaining asleep and can result in obscenely early morning awakening. Causative factors include stress, pain and underlying medical complications. In young children sleep anxiety is a common trigger.

Dealing with insomnia typically begins by understanding and minimising the stressors and developing a routine to reduce their impact.

Sleep Related Breathing Disorders

Sleep related breathing disorders are categorised by their influence on an individual's breathing. There are a host of variations, the most common of which is Obstructive Sleep Apnea. It is also the most serious.

Obstructive Sleep Apnea (OSA)

As the name suggests, OSA affects those afflicted by obstructing airways affecting one's breathing. Typically the relaxation of muscles in the upper airway when asleep results in the collapse of tissue at the back of the throat. Alternatively, the tongue may recede when asleep on the back. Either way, the obstruction limits the amount of air that can reach the lungs.

If you know someone who has OSA, you're probably aware of their proneness to snoring loudly or making choking noises as they battle airway restriction. More serious than the audible impact is the deprivation of oxygen to the brain causing waking, sometimes hundreds of times a night, although in most instances those affected are unaware.

This terribly broken sleep can have a profound impact on daytime functioning, leaving you drowsy, fatigued and struggling to concentrate. You may find yourself drifting off at inopportune moments, even if you believe you've had a full night's sleep.

OSA can occur in children. An estimated 2% of young children experience sleep apnea requiring medical intervention. The relative size of tonsils and adenoids to the throat makes this particularly prevalent in pre-schoolers. Sleep apnea has been linked to bedwetting, behavioural and learning difficulties, hyperactivity and ADHD, alongside abnormal growth and development.

The good news for parents is that the arousal threshold is higher in children than adults rendering kids less likely to wake frequently with pauses in breathing. In most cases kids will also adjust their position to respond to airway obstructions. Excessive daytime sleepiness is also more common in adults with OSA.

Infant Sleep Apnea

While even healthy infants can have irregularities in breathing patterns and short apneas, infant sleep apneas can result in consequential health issues due to the lowered concentration of oxygen in the blood. Typically these are a developmental problem caused by an immature brainstem or a secondary medical problem.

Infants can suffer from obstructive, central or mixed apneas. Obstructive apneas are consistent with the OSA discussion above. Central apneas occur when the body reduces or ceases its effort to breathe. This is driven from a brain or heart complication as opposed to an obstruction. Mixed apneas, as you could imagine, are a combinations of the two, commonly a central apnea followed by an obstructive apnea.

Central Sleep Apnea (CSA)

Adults also suffer brain or heart problems causing central sleep apneas, characterised by an off and on breathing cycle. A central sleep apnea can fall into one of the following categories: Primary Central Sleep Apnea, Cheyne Stokes Breathing Pattern, Medical Condition Not Cheyne-Stokes, High Altitude Periodic Breathing, Drug or substance abuse.

It's probably quite clear that the latter two categories of CSA are encouraged when sleeping at high altitudes, or through the use of certain drugs, most commonly within the Opioid family. The other three CSA varieties are caused primarily via a diagnosed medical condition such as heart failure, stroke or kidney complications and are categorised by the presence or absence of a rhythmic breathing pattern.

Snoring

While I like to believe I don't snore myself, snoring is extremely common. Most people snore from time to time, although they may not even realise it unless they receive a prod from an agitated partner. Light snoring may not impact sleep quality. Heavy snoring on the other hand can be more than simply a nuisance for anyone within earshot. Snoring is linked to a variety of sleeping disorders and can be a risk factor for other health problems.

About 10% of kids snore regularly. I mentioned the impact large tonsils or adenoids plays in sleep apnea. This also causes general snoring. Nasal congestion is also a key contributor. In the majority of instances snoring has limited impact on a child's daytime performance, although at times it can facilitate changes to a child's sleep cycle - enabling restlessness, regular awakenings and impacting your child's mood.

Sleep Related Groaning

Does your partner make a prolonged groaning sound during sleep exhalation? Thankfully, Catathrenia, or sleep related groaning, is a relatively rare sleep disorder more common in men than women. Groaning can be frequent, quite loud, and last a few moments to longer than 40 seconds. It often ends with an audible grunt or sigh.

Patients usually remain unaware; partners on the other hand get quite concerned! The cause is currently unknown although sleep related groaning is potentially related to restless sleep and subsequent daytime fatigue.

Hypersomnolence: Central Disorders

Hypersomnolence central disorders are unique in that despite achieving what experts term sufficient quality and length of sleep, sufferers still encounter severe daytime drowsiness. Those afflicted are compelled to nap repeatedly, despite achieving little respite from their symptoms. Sleeping can occur at highly inopportune or inappropriate times such as in the middle of a work meeting.

The excessive sleepiness can hang around for several months inflicting disorientation and difficulty waking. Anxiety, low energy, a loss of appetite and memory are also common symptoms. There are three main types of hypersomnolence central disorders - narcolepsy type 1, narcolepsy type 2, and idiopathic hypersomnia (IH). They typically affect adolescents and young adults and it appears there may be a genetic predisposition, although little is known about the causative factors.

Physical problems such as tumors, trauma, central nervous injury, or medical complications such as Multiple Sclerosis, depression and epilepsy have all been associated with these types of sleep disorders.

Circadian Rhythm Sleep-Wake Disorders

Stemming from the Latin interpretation 'around the day', the circadian rhythm is a 24-hour cycle of physiological processes that humans adhere to. Otherwise known as our internal body clock, the circadian rhythm is responsible for regulating the cycle of biological processes and is influenced and modulated by external cues such as sunlight exposure and temperature.

Circadian rhythm sleep-wake disorders are disturbances to our body's internal rhythm. They may be occasional disruptions but can equally cause ongoing alterations to sleep patterns. Characterised by a lack of congruence between the external environment and internal body clock, they are often linked to insomnia, excessive sleepiness and social impairment.

Circadian Sleep Disorders include the following:

• **Delayed sleep phase syndrome.** Sufferers fail to fall asleep until very late at night and as a result tend to sleep late into the morning or early afternoon.

• **Non 24 hour sleep wake disorder.** This is a condition where an individual possesses a body clock longer than the typical 24 hours. Accordingly they experience progressively later sleep times, eventually sleeping during the day until their cycle resets itself.

• **Advanced sleep phase syndrome.** Patients with this particular complaint seem to follow the often coined phrase 'early to bed, early to rise...' They are compelled to sleep far earlier than normal and wake extremely early in the morning.

• **Irregular sleep wake disorder.** 'Irregular' is the key phrase here. Patients may participate in several sleep periods per day, with non-uniform sleep and wake times.

• **Shift work disorder.** I have always thought shift work would be really tough. This condition is a work induced change in circadian rhythm where the patient experiences extreme difficulty in adjustment.

Parasomnias

As a mother or father to young children parasomnias are sleep disorders you may be exposed to. They are typically highly disruptive, yet less frequent sleep related events. Parasomnias include teeth grinding, night terrors, nightmares, sleepwalking and bed wetting. I would like to touch on a few of these.

Nightmares

Does your child frequently arrive in your room visibly shaken, complaining of a bad dream. Nightmares are relatively common, but can be extremely frightening for a child, occurring predominantly during REM sleep. Once a child hits toddler age they begin active dreaming but struggle to separate reality from imagination. A stressful or emotional occurrence during the day can find its way into nightmares in the evening.

While they can really scare a small toddler or child, a short period of comfort is usually sufficient to settle nerves and encourage your child back to bed.

Night Terrors

Although similar in name, night terrors are distinctly different from nightmares. Night terrors occur earlier in the sleep cycle and during non REM sleep. They are typically more alarming for parents as they are associated with screaming, thrashing of arms and legs, violent behaviour, and confusion.

Despite the distress you may feel witnessing your child go through night terrors, your child should settle relatively quickly and without memory of the incident. Comforting is not normally recommended or helpful as children are still asleep when they experience these sleep disruptions.

"Confusion arousal night terrors" are a variant of night terrors in toddlers and older infants. They are characterised by a gradual escalation in groaning to crying out, followed by increasingly violent behaviours. Standard night terrors are usually more acute onset.

With any night terror incident it is important to ensure your child's wellbeing, checking their room is free from hazards that might compromise safety. There are some sleep specialists who believe night terrors are related to sleep deprivation, fatigue or stress. Maintaining normal sleep patterns may help minimise the onset of night terrors for your child.

Bedwetting

Bed wetting is extremely common. You probably don't even consider this a sleep disorder, merely a side effect of toilet training. For most, bed wetting is confined to toddler or preschool years, although it can continue well into primary or elementary school. Generally a child will outgrow it and there is nothing to worry about. Sometimes there is a family history of bed wetting, poor bladder control or developmental lag.

Bed wetting can be caused by anxiety or emotional distress and in rare cases has been linked to allergy or infection. It is also associated with obstructive sleep apnea. Bed wetters sometimes experience daytime drowsiness through reductions in sleep quality, although ordinarily the disruption to sleep of bed wetting is more frustrating for parents than children!

Sleep-Related Movement Disorders

Is your child moving excessively during their sleep? You're probably thinking - what a ridiculous question! Or course they are, the covers are sprayed everywhere and I seem to tuck them in multiple times every evening.

Sleep related movement disorders can be extremely difficult to establish as you can imagine. These problems are categorised by movement during or before sleep, making it difficult to drift off to sleep, or remain that way. Daytime sleepiness, insomnia and a failure to achieve quality restorative sleep is common due to body movements.

Motion could include short limb twitches, leg cramps or general restlessness, but shouldn't be confused with the standard jerking movement most people exhibit when falling to sleep.

• **Restless leg syndrome.** If your child complains of legs falling asleep, or a burning, itching or crawling sensation inside their legs when prone then they may be experiencing restless leg syndrome. This disorder occurs when awake, is particularly uncomfortable, and makes it extremely difficult to sleep. Symptoms usually abate when standing up or moving around.

• **Periodic limb movements.** These are linked to the sensation of uncontrollable and repetitive muscle movements, most often in the lower legs. It can be persistent throughout the night and severely impact quality of sleep.

• **Sleep leg cramps.** Most individuals have suffered the sudden and intense pain associated with cramp, either on the sports field or during a recreational pursuit. The sudden contraction and tightening of muscle causing pain occurs during sleep leg cramps as well. They can occur while awake or after you have fallen asleep.

• **Sleep rhythmic movement.** Does your toddler make a constant banging noise while seemingly asleep? This may be their body moving but often it could be associated with banging their head against the cot or another object. You may wonder if your child understands the pain they are inflicting - but it could be that they are experiencing sleep rhythmic disorder - characterised by repeated body movements while drowsy or asleep.

What If My Child Has a Sleeping Disorder?

Are you concerned your tired, grumpy or poorly behaved child is the output result of a sleeping disorder? Are you at your wits end trying to encourage your child to sleep through the night? Or are you faced with ongoing sleep disturbances, bed wetting, terrors, snoring or general restlessness?

Sleeping problems are widespread in infants, toddlers and preschool children. Most often these problems can be resolved with specific interventions. If your toddler is simply not sleeping well, or it is a battle every night to get him or her to sleep, then we will talk about how to manage this in a couple of chapters, so please read on.

If however, some of the signs and symptoms we referred to in the aforementioned sleep disorders ring true and you believe there is something more serious at play, I suggest you get medical assistance from your child's doctor or paediatrician. If nothing else it will provide much needed peace of mind. If nothing untoward is at play, then you can move on with some of the behavioural suggestions covered later in this book.

Chapter 3
Stages Of Sleep

Overview of Stages of Sleeping

I hope the previous chapter has provided a reasonable understanding of the importance of sleep and how it applies to both you as a parent and your precious baby or toddler.

While I probably sound a bit like a broken record by now, sleep is of utmost importance. Though it's worth mentioning not all sleep is the same. It might appear the process of sleeping is consistent every night... get your toddler into bed, perhaps read a few pages of a popular bedtime story, flick off the light switch and watch them drift off blissfully to sleep (if only...), then observe as they wake bright eyed and bushy tailed in the morning.

However, there's much more to it than that. When you sleep there are a large number of physiological changes occurring throughout the body, and these transpire during different stages of sleep.

These so-called sleep phases do not draw a linear pattern. Sleep is a gradual progression. The process builds and cycles throughout the night-time hours associated with remarkable bodily changes.

Circadian Rhythms and Sleep

Prior to entering the all-important sleep cycle your toddler needs to actually drift off to sleep! Falling asleep is a measured and often tumultuous process. Snuggling into bed with the light off and eyes closed does not necessarily fast track the process. It often seems the more you focus on sleep the less likely it will occur. How do we get to sleep? A wide range of hormones, chemicals and regions of the brain interact to transition from wide awake to the beginning of a toddler's sleep cycle.

Responsibility for altering the state of arousal falls upon something called neurotransmitters. What are neurotransmitters? They are chemicals that interact with specific neurons or nerve cells within the brain. Interactions can alter the level of wakefulness or alertness. Serotonin and norepinephrine are two such neurotransmitters whose role is to ensure the brain remains active when awake.

Adenosine is another chemical critical to the sleep cycle. Scientists believe adenosine accumulates in the blood throughout the period of waking, causing drowsiness. Once asleep, levels of adenosine decline. Research suggests that the reduction in adenosine then prompts us to wake, since the body no longer requires sleep to complete the chemical breakdown.

I mentioned earlier that cortisol is a well-recognised stress hormone. Interestingly, the level of cortisol in your body also fluctuates throughout the day. Cortisol progressively decreases towards the evening to allow relaxation from daily stresses and encouraging sleep. It then increases during the night to prepare for the morning, rendering you alert and rearing to go. An inability to reduce stress and thus cortisol levels can impact one's ability to drift off to sleep. I discussed briefly in the last chapter the concept of the 'body clock'. Just to recap slightly, the internal body clock is responsible for controlling your circadian rhythms - the cycle of physiological processes (both mental and physical) throughout the day. Accordingly it plays a critical role in successfully managing sleep schedules.

Your circadian rhythm rises and falls at various times of day impacting your level of alertness. Encouragingly, if you have achieved sufficient sleep, daily circadian dips are generally less intense.

So, what exactly is this internal body clock? Is it simply a concept? Actually it refers to a small area of pinhead sized brain structures referred to as the suprachiasmatic nucleus or SCN. They are located in the brain's hypothalamus and are influential in the release of the hormone melatonin.

Light information from the eyes travels courtesy of the optic nerve, eventually acting on the SCN. The SCN then instructs the pineal gland on when to release melatonin, a hormone scientists believe is responsible for turning off specific brain areas as we drift off to sleep. In the presence of adequate light, the SCN switches off production of melatonin. After dark however, we observe a sudden escalation in melatonin levels and a subsequent onset of drowsiness. Regulation of body temperature, blood pressure, urine production and hormone secretion are all influenced by our 'body clock' as we transition through various components of our sleep cycle.

It's not only the body clock and impact of light or dark that affects circadian rhythms. You can probably think of a number of external cues that disrupt our body's natural tempo. A baby crying out for attention during the early hours is an obvious one, an alarm clock blaring, for those with the luxury of sleeping through the night, another!

Stages Of Sleep

Humans typically progress through five defined stages of sleep. Stages one to four are classified as non REM sleep. Stage five is referred to as REM or rapid eye movement sleep.

The completion of five sleep stages is a cyclical process, the body transitioning through each stage every 15-20 minutes to complete a typical sleep cycle in 90-110 minutes. An individual will conclude several sleep cycles throughout the day or night as they accomplish the necessary sleep requirement.

The nature of the cycle alters significantly during the evening. Early on, REM sleep is relatively short, the body favouring restorative deep sleep, but as the process persists throughout your night-time slumber the body favours longer REM periods, reducing the length of deep sleep.

When bedtime rolls around, the lights are off and you or your toddler has let go of the day's events, you enter a period of quiet wakefulness accompanied by 'alpha' brain waves. Your brain is progressively disengaging with the world as thoughts oscillate between internal and external. As brain waves slow, and transfer from alpha to 'theta' band waves you enter transitional sleep.

Stage 1: Transitional sleep stage

Just as he or she drifts off to sleep, your toddler seems to be disrupted and woken easily. Why? During the initial stage of sleep eyes are closed, but sleep is particularly light. In fact the body actually drifts in and out of sleep during this phase. Transitional sleep may last between 5 and 10 minutes.

During transitional sleep eyes move slowly, muscle activity and brain waves (fluctuations of electrical activity in the brain) begin to slow. Have you felt the sense of falling as you drift off to sleep only to wake with a sudden jolt? This sensation and associated muscle contraction, referred to as hyping myoclonic, is common during the initial sleep stage.

Sleep experts believe every time humans fall asleep this jerky muscle contraction occurs. Apparently most people typically don't notice it. It's the larger more violent jerkiness we recall occurring when the body is exceptionally tired.

Interestingly, while technically sleep is underway during this stage - academic research has demonstrated a high proportion of individuals do not consider themselves asleep when woken from this phase.

Stage 2: Light sleep

From transitional sleep toddlers enter stage two, the light sleep phase. At this point they have lost awareness of surroundings and begin to complete a filtering process of the day's events. Eye movement stops, breathing slows, brain waves become even slower with a calmer brain pattern eventuating. Heart rate subsides and body temperature is lowered, in a similar way to how bears hibernate. Useless information picked up during the day's events is forgotten.

Toddlers can still be awakened relatively easily, although they are now preparing for stage three- deep sleep.

Stage 3: Entering deep sleep

Stage three and four are categorised as restorative sleep. This is a deep sleep stage. The kind of sleep you crave when immensely tired. The kind of sleep when you need an alarm clock to stop you sleeping forever!

During this stage breathing slows further, muscles relax, blood pressure continues to be lowered, as does body temperature. Throughout deep sleep toddlers exhibit the slowest of all brain waves, called delta waves, and the body begins regenerative work - repairing and regrowing tissues, constructing bone and muscle and strengthening immune function.

Deep sleep is a phase of sleep you love to see your baby in… resting peacefully without a care in the world. Waking a child during deep sleep will leave them disorientated. As we age, we sleep more lightly and achieve less deep sleep. Often (it seems) if you have young children in the household. However, many experts believe we still require the same amount of deep sleep as we get older.

Stage 4: Continuing deep sleep

If your toddler is difficult to rouse from their slumber, or wakes particularly groggy, struggling to adjust to their awakened state, chances are they were engaged in stage four- deep sleep. Similar to stage three, this phase features delta brain waves almost exclusively, and is characterised by no eye movement or muscle activity.

During stage four the regeneration process continues as the body repairs individual cells, not just brain cells. A lack of sleep can impact the entire body's recovery process. During stage four some children experience bedwetting, night terrors and sleep walking.

Deep, slow wave sleep occurs predominantly in the first half of the night. The second half is dominated by REM sleep.

Stage 5: Rapid eye movement sleep

The first four stages are referenced collectively as non REM sleep. The fifth and final stage of sleep is rapid eye movement sleep (REM). This all important phase was only discovered in 1953 with the introduction of new sleep analysis methods.

REM sleep is more active than the previous sleep stages and is characterised by eyes rapidly moving in different directions, a phenomenon not present in stages one to four. Individuals entering REM sleep experience fast, irregular and often shallow breathing, their blood pressure begins to rise again, as does heart rate. A person's ability to regulate temperature is also impacted during this phase.

REM sleep releases a sharp increase in brain waves, achieving levels similar to those exhibited when awake. However, despite this, sleep type showcasing the most active brain function of all stages, muscles remain temporarily paralysed during this time. With an active brain, REM sleep is the period of sleep that encourages dreaming, and sleep experts believe it holds a really important link to learning, memory and creativity. Dr Alon Y. Avidan, a professor of neurology at the UCLA Sleep Disorders Center suggests that during REM sleep "you're organising thoughts and learning, filing information" although he concedes there is much to learn about why the sleeping mind is active. When woken during REM sleep it is common to recall dreams in vivid detail. I love listening to my children recount stories of bizarre or illogical dreams. Scientists believe infants spent up to 50% of sleep duration in REM sleep. As we age we achieve progressively less REM sleep with adults spending only 20% of their night-time hours in REM, and half of their sleep in stage two.

Three to five intervals of REM sleep usually occur each night, the first of which is around 90 minutes after we drift off. The first cycle may last just 10 minutes, however throughout the night each period of REM sleep gets progressively longer, the last potentially continuing for up to an hour. As these periods of REM sleep increase there is a corresponding decrease in the duration of deep sleep, stages three and four. The sleep cycle becomes predominantly one, two and REM.

Chapter 4
How Much Sleep Do We Need?

The amount of sleep individuals need and the characteristics of sleep differ substantially, contingent on the stage of life and individual requirements.

Some babies would seemingly sleep through a rock concert while others wake at the slightest disturbance. Toddlers or slightly older children routinely resist sleep time, coming up with a multitude of excuses as to why they don't need to go to bed. A favourite of mine was the insistence of my three year old that her bed was 'stupid'.

We all know it is almost impossible to convince teens to switch off their mobile phone and go to sleep before the midnight hour and it's even harder to prompt them to rise from their slumber to ready themselves for school or to engage with the world.

I'm sure you've been exposed to the commonly held view that sleep before midnight is more important than the hours post-midnight. I am not 100% sure of the accuracy of this statement, although it makes sense if you consider the disruption to one's body clock.

A Decline In Sleep Volumes

I touched on this point earlier when discussing my story; there is increasing evidence of a decline in the amount of sleep both adults and children are achieving over the past couple of decades. Some experts suggest adult sleep volumes are likely to be around 7 hours or less, compared to a more substantial 8-8.5 hours back in the 60s and 70s.

Do we need less sleep? Unlikely. People are busier and more stressed than ever. The likelihood is we require more sleep to aid our recovery and to unwind.

Increasingly busy lives consisting of jobs, kids, recreational pursuits, technology and financial stresses means sleep is sometimes neglected in the all-important health equation. We spend up to a third of our life sleeping. While it's easy to consider this a waste of productivity... sleep is as vital as food, water and oxygen in maintaining health and wellbeing.

When chasing a deadline or attending to your toddler's every need, cutting back on sleep can seem like a logical and worthy trade-off. But even a slight reduction in sleep can impact mood, concentration and stress levels.

Toss into the mix the consumption of stimulants like coffee, coke, energy drinks; the use of alarm clocks and electronic devices; as well as inappropriate lighting, then you are messing with the body's natural rhythm and sleeping patterns. The result? You end up with sleep deprivation debt. I know I've probably over emphasized this point but I do believe very few of us remember what it is like to be truly rested. It took me a long time to recognise it again.

To understand the amount of sleep your mind and body need it is useful to comprehend where you fall on the sleep needs spectrum. It is also worthwhile reviewing elements of your lifestyle that may have a profound impact on sleep such as the volume, timing and quality of sleep you engage in.

I know this is easier said than done. Especially when parent to a young child who simply refuses to allow you the sleep you desire or deserve. I will discuss ways of t getting children to sleep and ensuring they remain asleep in the next chapter - for now I am simply considering elements of your circumstances (outside of demanding children) that could be influencing your sleeping habits.

Signs Of Excessive Sleepiness

We previously discussed some of the impacts of lack of sleep - from irritability and moodiness to dis-inhibition, flattened emotional responses, a lack of motivation, through to more serious ailments.

If you are not getting enough sleep then the likelihood is you'll become sleep deprived, either for a short period, or more long lasting. The realisation of how sleep deprivation is affecting you will often go unnoticed until you have caught up on sleep debt.

Have you forgotten what it's like to be bright eyed and bushy tailed in the mornings, ready to take on the challenges of the day? Is it normal for you to be fighting sleep in front of the TV or in the middle of the afternoon?

Let's touch on a few clear signs you might be sleep deprived or suffering excessive sleepiness:

• Without an alarm clock or smart phone you're likely to be late for work!

• The alarm clock or smart phone's snooze button gets a hammering

• Getting out of bed in the morning seems like the toughest part of the day

• You become fatigued and sluggish in the afternoon

• It is common for you to fight sleep in meetings, or warm rooms

• You want to curl up and go to sleep after a big meal

• A nap is an essential part of your day

• You frequently fall asleep in front of your favourite TV program

• You drift off as soon as your head hits the pillow

Myths about sleep

As with any important and perhaps misunderstood endeavour, there are a lot of myths or mistruths about sleep that circulate for both adults and children. Before we touch on the exact amount of sleep you should be getting, let's look at a few of the more popular sleep myths.

Myth 1: Losing an hour or two of sleep makes no difference to performance.

Unfortunately not. Losing as little as one hour's sleep can affect your ability to think clearly, respond or react quickly.

Myth 2: Keeping your baby up during the day will ensure they sleep longer at night.

This is a lovely thought but is not grounded in reality. Newborn babies have unorganised brains that are developing at a rapid pace. Sleep rhythms develop as these brains mature. Until they are 6-8 weeks old day or night is of little consequence to your baby boy or girl. There is a wise old saying – 'Sleep promotes sleep!'

The risks of keeping babies up for longer periods include the baby becoming overtired and an increase in cortisol production further impacting on their ability to sleep. While this may sound odd - babies and infants sleep better when they are well slept.

The concept of keeping children up for longer doesn't work particularly well with toddlers either. I'm sure you're familiar with the sight of your toddler running around in a hyperactive way when well past their bedtime. Often toddlers become more awake the more exhausted they get. Late nights can, and do impact on quality of sleep - leading to difficulty settling at night and regular night-time wakings.

Myth 3: Keeping your toddler awake later at night will provide you with a much needed sleep in.

The sleep-in you so desire might actually make for an earlier wake up in the morning due to an overtired child and disruptions to their circadian rhythm. A better alternative may be pushing for an earlier bedtime when toddlers are waking too early, particularly if your toddler or pre-schooler is getting less than 11-12 hours sleep at night.

Remember, changing sleep timings will not yield immediate results. You need to embed a new routine and establish the impact of any change over at least a week or so.

Myth 4: I am a terrible sleeper so my child probably will be too.

Just because you have trouble sleeping doesn't mean your kids will follow suit. Sleep is a skill and therefore can be learnt. Often, there are preconceived ideas on sleep transition from parent down to child. Generally, sleep issues are unrelated to genetics and the problem is your attitude. Is it time to break the myth that your family has an issue with sleep?

Myth 5: Never ever wake a sleeping baby.

The time when your toddler or baby is asleep can be blissful. A chance to put your feet up, catch up on household chores or engage in real adult conversation. Why would you want to ruin this?

I often hear the adage "don't wake a sleeping baby". Is there any truth to this? Possibly not. In many cases waking or capping an afternoon sleep can be useful to encourage improved overall sleep behaviours. Prolonged napping can interfere with bedtimes in the evening or trying to maintain a double nap schedule.

Myth 6: I can catch up on sleep on the weekend.

Are you struggling your way through the week, striving just to get to the weekend? You will make up for an entire week of deprived sleep courtesy of your toddler with one almighty catch up. Then it will be smooth sailing again right?

Unfortunately this is not really the case. While it can play a role in catching up on sleep debt... one solid sleep won't completely conquer your sleep deprivation, or overcome long term sleep inadequacy. This approach can also impact on your regular sleep wake cycle rendering it difficult to get to sleep Sunday evening, kicking you right back into sleep debt on Monday morning.

Don't get me wrong, temporary relief is certainly worthwhile. However, systematic improvements in sleeping patterns are more likely to ensure your performance and energy is maintained for the long term.

Myth 7: My child just doesn't need a lot of sleep.

Yes, the amount of sleep required varies between individuals. Some people can function well on less sleep than others. However, there are still basic sleep targets that you should aim for. We will touch on these targets really soon.

If your toddler's emotions are relatively steady, they are rarely sick, and learning and development is progressing well, then their sleep needs are probably in line with individual requirements.

Myth 8: Yawning is a sign of tiredness.

It's fair to say that yawning is not fully understood. A new study published in the Physiology & Behaviour journal has proposed yawning has nothing to do with tiredness, but is actually a mechanism to cool our brains and help us function more clearly.

But we yawn when we feel tired though? The researchers proposed that brain temperature is increased when you are tired or sleep deprived and yawns help regulate brain temperature as opposed to making us more awake.

Other researchers have proposed that yawning is related to changing conditions in the body such as when we are exhausted, awakening or at other periods when alertness levels are modified.

So indirectly, yawning can be related to tiredness.

Myth 9: Everyone needs at least 8 hours sleep a night.

Not necessarily. Babies, toddlers and children in general need a whole lot more. So do some adults. This leads us nicely into some statistics on the recommended volumes of sleep you should target for yourself and your toddler.

How much sleep does my toddler require?

While there is no substitute for high quality restorative sleep, my initial answer here is going to sound a little like a 'cop out'. There really is no right amount. The answer depends on individual differences and where you fall on a sleep continuum.

Take adults for example. Some individuals can function perfectly well on only six hours per night. Others are a write off unless they get a minimum of nine hours. Differences between individuals can be stark and are determined genetically and hereditarily. It's a tough balancing act getting enough sleep versus too much sleep.

Yes, there really is such a thing as getting too much sleep! In fact too much sleep has been associated with cognitive impairment, higher risk of obesity, diabetes, heart disease and stroke. Although researchers are quick to note that two other factors - low socio economic status and depression are strongly correlated with oversleeping.

Paying attention to your individual toddler's needs and assessing how they react to different amounts of sleep will go a long way to understanding their sleep requirements.

The same goes for your needs. Are you healthy, happy and productive on seven hours shut eye per night? Or can you not seem to get into top gear without a much longer rest? Do you rely on caffeine or energy drinks to get you through the day? Do you feel sleepy when driving? These and other questions about health and wellbeing must be answered before you can calculate the amount of sleep you need.

Now, despite the fact I have just told you that sleep is individual... not everyone needs the same... and so on; there are established age based guidelines to provide a ballpark figure to work from.

These guidelines were updated by the National Sleep Foundation in 2015 (sleepfoundation.org). The National Sleep Foundation (NSF) provides up-to-date sleep advice and is trusted by millions of individuals in America and worldwide. They are recognised as one of the leading voices of sleep health. The guidelines are the result of a rigorous scientific process analysing hundreds of published research studies. So what are the recommended sleep targets?

Newborn Babies

Newborn babies seem to sleep all day. And they should do. They are growing and developing quickly. Newborns require between 14 and 17 hours of sleep every day according to the NSF guidelines. It's not abnormal for some babies to sleep up to 20 hours per day, waking only to feed.

As you know, babies don't snooze like adults. Typically, they will sleep for a two to four hour period in the first few weeks. This constant waking is tough on parents or caregivers, but is completely normal for the baby as their circadian rhythm is not yet established.

After the first 6 weeks you might start to notice your babies sleep habits settling down and sleep periods extending. All going well they will start to overcome day/night confusion and elongate their sleep during the evenings.

Infants 6-12 Months

When a child reaches the milestone of six months they should achieve between 12 and 15 hours of sleep per night.

This range has recently been widened from 14-15 hours to recognise individual differences.

From 6 months onwards is a critical stage for embedding healthy sleeping habits as your baby becomes more predictable. At this point infants are capable of sleeping through the night (woohoo I hear you say!) Regular napping remains important during the day to establish your baby's rhythm, and typically a child will move from three daily naps to a two nap structure during this period.

Toddlers

11 to 14 hours sleep per day is recommended for toddlers, even though they typically drop to one nap per day at this stage. Unfortunately, many toddlers fail to achieve the minimum of eleven recommended hours, despite the National Sleep Foundation believing in most cases they need it.

Pre-Schoolers

The recommended sleep range for pre-schoolers was widened slightly in the latest set of guidelines and now sits at 10 to 13 hours per night. Many have dropped their daytime nap by this stage, increasing the importance of an early bedtime to secure the sleep volume they require.

School Age

The introduction of school adds an entirely different pattern and stressors into a child's daily routine. It is common for kids to be extremely tired as they come to terms with their new vocation. Kids need plenty of rest to maximise learning and to keep their emotions in check. 9 to 11 hours per night is the recommended range for primary aged children.

Adolescence

The shift from adolescence into young adulthood provides the most dramatic change in deep sleep and sleep satisfaction. A steep decline in deep slow wave sleep occurs throughout the teen years into the early twenties - replaced by stage two sleep.

Teenagers typically require between 8 and 10 hours of sleep per night. But you try telling them that...

Adulthood

It's a sad fact that as we age we get less sleep. We don't necessarily need or want less sleep... a bunch of factors just seem to get in the way.

What sort of factors get in the way of sleep for adults? Well children for one. They are an obvious driver of lack of sleep. But equally, many other sleep problems get worse with age. For men there is an increasing prevalence of sleep disorders as they pass through every subsequent decade of life. For women sleep patterns are pretty stable... until we have kids. Then comes the reality of pregnancy related lower back pain and stress anxiety that affects sleep. The arrival of bubs doesn't help... then sleeping patterns go haywire for a few years.

And just as you have the kids out the door and on their own in the world... and are eagerly awaiting a well-rested existence - menopause kicks in and incidence of many sleep disorders increase, the prevalence becoming more or less equivalent to men.

Even when you hit your senior years and seemingly have all the time in the world for sleep, doctors believe seniors are still not getting all the sleep they require. The frequent sleep on the sofa in front of daytime TV doesn't make up for a lack of satisfying and restorative sleep at night.

To some extent issues of ageing such as back or hip complaints affect sleep patterns. Experts also believe ageing can throw circadian rhythms off - encouraging grandpa to go to bed early, wake up early and potentially unlearn sleep structures.

The average adult requires between 7.5 and 8 hours of sleep per night. For younger adults the recommended range is slightly wider from 7 to 9 hours and seniors need between 7 and 8 hours sleep every evening.

Chapter 5
Getting Your Child to Sleep

Why Is It So Difficult?

Encouraging your child into healthy sleep habits is one of the most influential things you can do for their wellbeing. But do they appreciate it? Certainly not! So, why is it 'oh so difficult' to convince your toddler to get into bed, stay there, and drop off into a well-earned deep sleep?

A gentle resistance to bed or sleep can start off as incredibly endearing. But, the novelty soon wanes on overtired parents. After a handful of nights you're at your wits end battling your pint sized adversary. This can go on for months on end, although I don't need to remind you of this I'm sure.

Even if you are triumphant early and successfully navigate your child into their room or bed this is only part of the struggle. Convincing a toddler to remain there can be demanding. Does your child constantly slide out of bed and roam the house?

Many parents experience a moment of pure joy as their bustling boy or girl drifts off to sleep for the night, providing a few hours kid free or personal time in the evening. But all too often parents suffer the consequences of an inability to self-settle, frequent waking, crying or calling out for mum or dad.

67

Does any of this sound familiar to your household? Do you eventually break and indulge your child with extra attention or a 'few' bonus minutes with the adults? Or, do your child's needs devastate your best laid plans as you welcome them into your bed simply to allow them, or you, to get some form of rest?

Establishing meticulous processes to encourage high quality sleep is really important. I've mentioned several times the influence of sleep deprivation on emotional control, hyperactivity, behavioural problems and learning difficulties. But how do you overcome an extraordinarily strong willed child to furnish them with the sleep they desperately need?

I'd like to provide some positive news at this point. Falling asleep is a skill almost all kids can learn. Yes, for some, learning this skill is more gruelling than others. Although, even the most difficult child can evolve their sporadic sleeping structure into a well formed habit…it may just take a little longer.

I like to think I'm testament to the truth of even the worst sleeping toddlers can be remedied. Once you stumble on the right approach, add a little time and effort, and mix in an element of steely resolve, sleeping children can be the outcome. You shouldn't need to resort to bribery, co-sleeping, constant supervision or any other sneaky tricks you have in mind. Imagine how life would change if your child put themselves to sleep and stayed that way until morning (sigh…).

Common Behavioural Challenges

Before we delve into exactly how to approach this seemingly impossible task, let's quickly list a few common problems that surface at sleep time. They are many and various, but here is a snapshot of the more prevalent ones:

Bedtime Battles: No More!

• Your toddler puts on a performance Dame Judi Dench would be proud of whenever you mention the word 'bedtime'

• You encounter stern resistance to entering the bedroom or getting into bed

• As soon as you sit down to relax in the other room your child surfaces seeking attention

• Your boy or girl begins roaming their room playing with every truck, trailer, Barbie or Ken doll in the toy box, unpacking drawers, or dressing up in their favourite superhero costume

• Banging onto the side of the cot seems a logical way to get mum or dad's attention and to lure them back to their room

• Your infant or toddler has an inability to self-settle, craving comfort and assistance in order to drop off to sleep

• Even once you get your child to close their eyes they sleep for a short period of time only to wake again

• Constant waking throughout the night or obscenely early the next morning becomes routine

• You notice your toddler sneaking into the bed beside you in the middle of the night

• And finally, constant calling or crying out for mum or dad becomes a nightly or hourly occurrence

Sound familiar? So, that is a quick summary of some of the tactics your child is implementing to avoid sleep, or perhaps the behaviours that have been conditioned in your child at bedtime. The constant attention seeking, getting up, calling out or general troublemaking can be infuriating and the cause of much household conflict.

The problem is… sometimes your child does legitimately need assistance. They may actually be really thirsty, perhaps they are cold and unable to re-adjust their covers, they could have soiled themselves, or maybe they are suffering separation anxiety which is a common issue for children between 8 and 18 months old.

Just as the boy who cried wolf lost all credibility, the difficulty is in understanding when children are in need, and when they are playing a fantastic game of keeping parents around at bed time.

Excuses, excuses excuses…

Even when it was clear my children were testing me at bedtime it was often entertaining hearing some of the creative excuses they came up with to prolong the bedtime hour.

Here are a few of my favourites:

• I'm scared – "there are monsters in my room"

• I'm sick (when not actually sick]

• I don't want to go to sleep

• I'm not tired

• My leg / arm/ stomach / finger (you name it) hurts… I need a Bandaid

• I can't find my teddy

• I can't sleep without…

• I'm hungry…

• I'm thirsty…

• I forgot to tell you something…

• You forgot to give teddy a kiss

• I'm hot… or… I'm cold

• You forgot to…

• I need to go to toilet [again]

While some of these are more creative than others, and you may commend your child for their endeavour… it is important to stay strong against the barrage of excuses even when they are endearingly cute. But it is not just kids making excuses for poor bedtime habits. Parents are often just as guilty of absolving responsibility for their kid's substandard sleeping patterns. Parents often convince themselves that enforcing changes to sleep habits is against the toddler's best interests.

Some popular excuses parents make include:

• My child is teething

Have you decided to stop your regular or attempted sleep routine because your child is getting new teeth? Granted, for some infants or toddlers this can be a painful and disruptive experience that plays havoc with their mood, eating and sleeping structure. However, should you hold off engaging in sleep training or modify their bedtime routine to allow for teeth to come through? The short answer is no.

It's important to continue to prioritise your child's sleep. Babies and toddlers get new teeth over a period of months and even years. If you alter their routine or cease sleep training every time they are acquiring new teeth you'll never get them in a settled process. Yes, there might be a little more fussing, drooling and comforting along the way, but don't let that derail your efforts to develop a consistent practice.

• My child has been unwell

If your toddler has been sick, congested, coughing or spluttering then making a few exceptions for their sleeping behaviour is understandable and acceptable... while they are sick. Perhaps they will nap slightly longer during the day, affecting their normally strict bedtime. But these deviations should be short lived.

It is common for parents to make excuses for days or weeks following a bout of illness, by which time a toddler's sleeping routine has been severely compromised. I have certainly been guilty of this in the past.

• They are undergoing a growth spurt

Sometimes parents blame a growth spurt for irregular sleeping habits. The thought that their child wakes up hungry and needs food to support sudden growth seems to tie in with this theory.

Interestingly, a research study documented in the 2011 journal Sleep revealed an increase in total daily hours of sleep and sleep sessions when an infant was experiencing a growth spurt. This seems to contradict the parental theory a lack of, or irregular, sleep is the result of a growth spurt.

• Sleep isn't really an issue

A common remark from parents I talk to is that sleep isn't really an issue for their child...that they get plenty of sleep so it's not really a problem. Really? Often a toddler's behaviour will suggest otherwise.

At one stage I tried to convince myself of this as well. If parents are honest with themselves, or take the time to audit their child's sleep volume and quality, they will probably realise it's time to confront their toddlers irregular sleep patterns. Making excuses for a child is typically the result of a resistance to tackle sleep related issues head on, even if they have a reasonable inkling there may be a problem requiring attention.

However, sometimes parents unknowingly or unwittingly make parenting mistakes that impact their baby or toddler's sleep performance. Let's look at some of the most common mistakes parents make as they endeavour to get their child to sleep through the night.

Common Mistakes Parents Make

Babies don't settle into strong circadian rhythms until they are about three months old. Some take a lot longer. Armed with the knowledge that sleep is vitally important it's easy to take shortcuts to encourage sleep to the detriment of long term patterns. Helping your baby start to tune its internal clock in the first few months after birth is extremely valuable.

Early on, your involvement might be as simple as instituting appropriate social cues about day and night, exposing them to sunlight during the day and avoiding bright lights in the evening. However, if you start off making mistakes with your baby at bedtime, these are commonly carried through to toddler age.

If you aren't aware of this already... you'll soon come to realise the toddler years are already fraught with sleep disruptions. You don't need to add any of your own creations into the mix!

On a positive note, whether your child's sleep problems are recently developed issues or something you've previously encouraged that has come back to bite you, with a bit of hard work and perseverance they can be consigned to the past.

Here are a few of the all too prevalent bedtime mistakes parents make with babies and toddlers. If you are having ongoing difficulty settling your child into a deep restorative sleep chances are you are making at least some of these mistakes:

• Absence of a bedtime routine

Does your baby or toddler have a defined sleeping routine or do you try to take a very relaxed approach with your child in the evening, putting them to bed when they are 'ready'?

Skipping or absence of a bedtime routine is a key driver of toddler sleep problems. In fact, a 2015 research study by Mindell et al investigating bedtime routines for young children found a consistent bedtime routine was associated with significantly improved sleep outcomes including earlier bedtimes, reduced night wakings and longer sleep durations in children aged 0 to 5 years.

Allowing your child time to wind down and relax before being placed in their cot or bed can make a substantial difference to the ease at which they settle and the quality of their sleep.

I know sometimes this can feel really rigid. The key is developing a strategy that integrates into your lifestyle but also achieves the goals of preparing your child for his or her slumber. This can become a wonderful bonding time for you and your child, quietly reading books and analysing the day's events.

• Not sticking with the sleep schedule

Perhaps you have a sleep time routine, but just fail to implement it on occasion…. at night or nap time, consistency is the key. Babies and toddlers require unchanging sleeping behaviours in order to regulate day and night hormone cycles and set internal body clocks.

Ensuring you baby goes to bed and sleep at a similar time every day is important. Constant change will impact your child's ability to cope. A common error is a bedtime that is too early when toddlers are not ready to sleep and likely to get up to mischief. A bedtime that is too late is just as troublesome. You want your child to be ready for bed but not overtired. A key consideration is ensuring nap times are not too late in the afternoon and are not for too long as this can impact on the quality of sleep throughout the evening.

Now, just to reiterate what I said earlier, I am not suggesting you need to follow your routine to the letter of the law, or condition bedtime to the exact minute. I understand that some flexibility is important. There will be times when routines need to be modified… but this should be the exception rather than the rule.

• Ignoring tell-tale signs your toddler is tired

Does it seem like your child is trying to tell you something with his or her constant whining, fighting with siblings or general demeanour in the evening? That's probably because they are. Children provide a range of tell-tale signs indicating they are tired and should be asleep. Eye rubbing, yawning, whining and fussing are but a few of them.

It's really vital you don't overlook these signs and miss the window of opportunity to get them to settle into bed. Too late will mean their all-important melatonin production will be overshadowed by cortisol build up. The result: an over tired and over stimulated child. Once that toddler gets a second wind it could be closer to midnight before you can reign him or her in again!

• Overstimulating your child before bedtime

A few fun games, exercises or interactions with your child are tempting in the evening once kids are fed, bathed and in their pyjamas. Unfortunately, these should be avoided in the build-up to sleep or as part of your bedtime routine. Exciting games are like a red rag to a bull for your sympathetic nervous system - a component of your brain that plays a central role in keeping you alert.

Focus needs to be on reducing excitement levels and slowly relaxing at the end of a long day. Think quiet and calm, focus on reading books, and lower light, as you coax your toddler into a drowsy sleepy state.

The same rules apply when trying to settle babies or toddlers back to sleep after waking during the night. Minimise the fuss, limit social engagement, eye contact or interaction. Think dark... quiet... boring.

• Making sleep decisions in the middle of the night

Formulating new sleep strategies in the dark of the night is a classic but totally understandable parental mistake. When we are tired ourselves it's easy to throw hands in the air crying 'I can't take it anymore', opting for the path of least resistance. Often this means welcoming toddlers into the marital bed under the premise you might get more sleep than fighting with them. Little did you know you're creating a much bigger issue in the long run.

Not only is it important to have a well defined routine, it is equally vital that you stick to it, even during the hours of darkness. A couple of days sticking to the plan could make up for a lifetime (well months anyway) of poor sleep.

• Letting them stay up late, hoping they'll sleep in

I touched on this earlier when we examined some of the sleep myths that exist. While it seems like a good idea... in reality it can have disastrous reverberations.

• Too much screen time

The matter of too much TV, iPad or smartphone exposure is certainly not one your parents ever had to worry about. Using TV or devices as a babysitter is tempting, particularly in the evening to try to encourage toddlers to settle down. However, emerging evidence suggests that screen time may be having a significant negative impact on children's sleep.

A 2014 review by Hale and Guan identified consistent evidence that screen time was associated with poor quality and insufficient sleep for children. The researchers suggested device exposure was interrupting normal bedtime routines, cutting into the time they would ordinarily be preparing for bed. This had the impact of delaying bedtimes and providing a consequential reduction in overall sleep duration. Screen time was also analogous with delayed onset of sleep.

While it is sometimes easy for parents to plonk their toddler in front of their tablet for half an hour before bed to get some much needed quiet time rather than preparing your child for sleep, this could be having a negative impact on the quality of sleep they acquire.

(http://www.smrv-journal.com/article/S1087-0792(14)00081-1/abstract)

• Using bribery

Bribery has its place… I think. But, perhaps not at bedtime. I can still remember myself providing my two year old with toy after toy on the condition she remained in bed. However, children are very canny. Your crafty child will sniff out an opportunity and end up extorting you for more and more treats. Instead, look to reinforce positive behaviours such as "I'm proud of you for staying in bed".

• Switching from cot to big-kid bed too early

Ah, I remember this all too well. In our case we felt we had little choice due to the size of our toddler in relation to her cot. Don't fall into the same trap if you can avoid it. When a child is too young to obey verbal instructions, such as staying in bed, the cot provides a useful barrier. When they are a bit older and ready for the big bed, they are less likely to roam the house. At least that is the theory anyway.

Of course, if your child is beginning to clamber out of the cot on their own accord it's time to consider new sleeping arrangements! They could cause serious harm as they throw themselves over the edge to escape to freedom.

• Putting him or her to sleep wherever you are

"I am not going to let my baby dictate my life, she needs to fit in with my lifestyle"… I seem to remember saying this to myself a few years ago. While it is true in that no-one wants to be a slave to their children's sleep, you do want your child to sleep properly. The odd rest in a car seat or stroller might be ok, but be warned that movement can impact on your child's ability to fall into deep restorative sleep.

It is important to provide your toddler with a familiar sleep zone for both naps and bedtime. Where possible, work around sleeps for appointments and social engagements.

Secure a babysitter if you are going out late in the evening. Too much sleeping in unfamiliar territory will compromise your sleep routine.

• Staying with your toddler until they fall asleep

It often feels like a wonderful time as a mother lying beside your precious toddler as they slowly drift off to sleep, rubbing his or her back, stroking their hair. The reality is that this is potentially harming your toddler's ability to settle without parental assistance. All of a sudden you find yourself lying in your child's tiny bed every evening and throughout the night just to get them to sleep again.

• Mum and dad aren't on the same page

"United we stand... divided we fall" the Brotherhood of Man song goes. The same is true for parenting. Parents need a united front when it comes to managing their baby or toddler's sleep issues.

Much like a military operation, tactics need to be agreed upon in advance, and both parents need to avoid deviation from these tactics. The big decisions are key. On what conditions do you enter the child's room? What is the process upon entry? Should you use sleep associations (more on this in a minute)? A lengthy discussion will ensure you are both on the same page at the outset. It might even pay to document your procedure. One parent can easily and unknowingly undermine the hard work of the other. Consistency is imperative in developing sleep behaviours. Communicate the basics of your sleep process with anyone else (grandparents etc) who may be looking after your precious bundle at bed time.

• **Giving up too soon**

When parents are sleep deprived and feel like they have been battling strong willed children for hours, giving up is easy. Patience is really vital in overcoming undesirable sleep habits. Reassuringly, it's never too late to overcome your toddler's issues. Just don't expect immediate results. Progress may take several days or weeks but once you see noteworthy changes it is worth it. Trust me!

Many parents fall into the all too common trap of enduring a couple of nights of limited sleep, combating tears, tantrums and turbulence with their child and immediately think this is all too hard. They cling to the hope that their child will modify their routine on their own when the time is right.

Don't give up too easily. A short bout of sleep deprivation is worth it for a lifetime of high quality rest!

• **Too quick to intervene**

As a parent it is customary to be anxious about the wellbeing of your toddler. But do you find yourself reacting to the slightest noise from your baby's cot, crib or bed? A frequent error effecting parents is reacting immediately when a child cries out, when in many cases they are actually still asleep.

Ignoring this brief interruption and waiting it out will allow them the opportunity to self-settle. If you race into their room like a bullet you might find you're the reason your child is fully awake and requires re-settling.

• **You aren't consistent in your approach**

The pain and exhaustion of sleep deprivation can provide a crushing blow to your once comfortable daily life. When operating on a lack of shuteye, it's easy to find yourself

80

alternating between techniques to manage contorted sleep behaviours.

Switching from planned responses to ignoring your child altogether, followed by overcompensating with affection, is usual. This can be confusing for your infant or toddler and may actually compound sleep issues they are sustaining. A single consistent approach is recommended. Set expectations with your child and adhere to them. It's really easy to drop a few threats to attempt to control a specific behaviour, but what do you do when your child ignores them?

The answer is to implement consequences and follow through with them. The best way to ensure that your toddler never takes you seriously is to throw out idle threats and never back them up!

In doing so, it is important to maintain a calm and controlled demeanour. Be firm in the face of adversity but try to avoid losing your temper. Yes, easier said than done I know... it requires immense patience.

• Putting your child to sleep hungry

If your child is hungry it is a sure fire way to motivate them to wake during the night. Your chances of uninterrupted sleep are increased tenfold when your baby or toddler is well fed. Make sure they eat up on healthy foods before bedtime. A 'dream feed' for babies between ten and midnight is a common method breastfeeding mothers implement to prolong sleep duration.

• Letting your child fall asleep in your arms or anywhere except their bed

There is something special about a child drifting off to sleep in the loving arms of mum or dad. However, that remarkable feeling can be short lived when it becomes apparent the only way an infant or toddler will fall asleep is cradled by a parent. It is important that a child is allowed to settle by themselves. Try to avoid rocking them to sleep in your arms. It is more supportive to developing desired sleeping habits if they are in bed or their cot before they enter transitional sleep.

• Creating sleep crutches

When a parent or child is exhausted we'll try anything to get children to sleep right? It could be rocking, walking, singing, lying beside them, rubbing their back, stroking their hair... there are a multitude of techniques you've probably rolled out.

For a period of time I resorted to turning the vacuum cleaner on and leaving it in my daughter's room, as the sound of me cleaning had put her to sleep a couple of times previously! You too may have stumbled on some weird and wonderful approaches that were effective in settling your toddler to sleep on occasion. This probably seemed like a good thing at the time. But is it?

The problem with this however is that continually resorting to a sleep 'crutch' after a period of time prompts a child to learn this behaviour. What do I mean? Consider this example. If you let your toddler cry for 10 minutes before entering the room to rock them, what do you think they will do tomorrow? Probably cry for 10 minutes to get you to rock them. And the next day?

Over time, every time the child wakes they'll need that particular sleep crutch in order to drift off to sleep. Ideally you want to place your child in bed awake, but drowsy, allowing them to self-settle. If you find yourself making poor decisions due to sleep related fatigue it might be time for a partner or spouse to relieve you to maintain an effective routine.

Sleep Associations and How They Affect Sleep

Ok, I have just introduced the concept of creating sleep 'crutches'. I'd like to talk a bit more about this topic. Sleep 'crutches' are regularly used by parents when they're unable to encourage their child to sleep on their own. A broader term for something a child associates with falling asleep is a 'sleep association'.

The term 'sleep association' can include conditions, props and activities a child psychologically associates or links with the act of sleeping. It may be a special toy or blanket, their bedroom or cot, gentle rocking, a pacifier or dummy, even darkness or a nightlight.

It's not just toddlers or babies that have sleep associations either, we all do. Adults just don't pay a great deal of attention to the specific conditions we require when preparing for our slumber. Perhaps you must have two pillows to get to sleep, the light in the hallway needs to be turned off, or you can't seem to sleep without unwinding at the hands of a good book.

Now just let me clarify one point. Sleep associations are distinctly different to the concept of a bedtime routine. A bedtime routine consists of activities involved in the process of getting to bed. If an element is related to the task of falling asleep it is considered a sleep association.

How Babies Learn Sleep Associations

Babies begin to learn sleep associations within just a few days or weeks of birth. How is this? Well, the most basic form of learning is by association. When a baby or toddler is exposed to repetition they form a connection. For example, if your child is repeatedly put to sleep the same way... they begin to link sleep to the process by which they are encouraged to sleep.

Ongoing exposure serves only to strengthen the process or the behaviour. How your baby is put to sleep can become their preferred way to sleep… or the only way they will settle. Is this wrong? Well, not if you have been conditioning your child to sleep in a desirable and sustainable manner.

In many cases you may not even recognise that you have been conditioning your toddler to sleep using certain actions. Moving forward, the actions you then take (or don't take) may encourage or discourage your child's sleeping.

From just a few weeks or months after birth it is favourable to make a conscious effort to teach the sleep associations you want your baby to rely on. Otherwise, the sleep associations they acquire may be less appealing, such as sleeping in your bed, rocking them to sleep every night or similar. Are sleep associations good or bad? It depends.

Does your toddler have a sleep toy? What happens if you head away for a well-deserved holiday and leave their precious snuggly toy behind? All hell breaks loose right? The related stress for both child and parents is immeasurable!

The problem with sleep associations is that babies and toddlers become accustomed to needing their particular association and you then are then forced to recreate these each and every time they sleep. If a sleep association is absent, they don't know how to get to sleep. If they wake they require the association periodically throughout the night.

You want your toddler to settle by themselves, but if they roll over and realise their dummy is gone, rocking has stopped, or mum and dad are no longer present… they resist falling asleep again, and all of a sudden are jolted wide awake, crying or calling out for your help.

I found myself lying beside my toddler periodically throughout the night in order to get her to sleep. Admittedly it eventually allowed my toddler to drift off to sleep - but it didn't do much for the quality of mine. Particularly when I found myself up and down every few hours after she woke. I still cringe when I think of it.

Before you know it your toddler or baby takes longer and longer to get to sleep or wakes up all night, even when a particular sleep association is present.

So, sleep associations may not start out as a bad thing... but they can become entrenched behaviour quickly when mismanaged. On what sleep props does your toddler rely? Identifying the sleep associations your child has created allows you to understand what is impacting your toddler's ability to sleep. There are countless sleep associations your child might resonate with from a simple cot or bed, to a range of sleep props such as rocking, feeding, co-sleeping and more.

Sleep props, a subset of sleep associations if you like, are little sleep addictions kids cannot control themselves. A glaring example is a parent or caregiver coming in to assist with settling them the entire time.

Sleep props interfere with a child's sleeping performance. How? Primarily because if they are even partially aroused from their sleep, they will be unable to drift off again unless their sleep prop is present.

Let's consider some of the more common sleep props:

• Physical contact with a parent such as cuddling or lying beside them as they fall asleep

• Being fed to sleep either via breast or bottle

• Rocking, patting or stroking

- Movement to encourage sleep - for example in a car or pacing the room

- Blankets that don't stay put or a specific type of covering

- Noise - shushing, singing or whispering

- Sucking on a dummy or pacifier

- Reactive co-sleeping

- Cuddling a bedtime toy

- A mobile that plays for a short period of time

The key to sleep associations is avoiding anything that the child can't control themselves. If there is a prop or aide that you wish to use for your child it must be there for them when asleep or awake, regardless of the time of day or night. If it isn't... they will no doubt want it!

A good example of this is a dummy or pacifier. Granted, many parents find it a useful sleep aide. Others find it an absolute nightmare, requiring countless trips to the bedroom throughout the night to reapply it to a toddler's mouth.

If a baby is unable to locate the dummy and re-administer it - this can create a negative sleep association. To circumvent continued wakings you either need to teach your baby to do it themselves - or remove the sleep prop altogether. Now, before you decide to simply 'wait it out' to see if your child's little sleep prop addiction goes away... I'm sorry to be the bearer of bad news. Sleep prop addictions don't usually vanish by themselves, in fact they often worsen over time. Act now!

How Sleep Associations Affect a Child's Sleep

Babies and small toddlers don't have the luxury of taking themselves off to bed when they're tired or recreating the conditions they prefer to sleep in. They rely heavily on a caregiver for this process.

The absence of accustomed sleep associations can have a profound impact on how easily a child falls asleep. Fussing, crying or screaming is recurrent until sleep conditions are comfortable as in the realm of their understanding.

The removal of a sleep association is not typically apparent during deep sleep... but when the toddler's cycle through to lighter stage one and two of sleep they may become aware of a change.

There are number of impacts the absence of a sleep association can have on your child's sleep:

• Propensity to remain awake with the risk of becoming overtired

• An overall reduction in quantity and quantity of sleep

• Risk of waking sooner or prematurely in the morning

• An accumulation of sleep debt over time

• Unfavourable behavioural changes associated with overtired toddlers

• An increase in your toddler's level of fatigue

Eventually the hours of whining, fussing and crying will end when exhaustion overpowers your youngster and they doze off, perhaps forgetting about the sleep associations they so dearly craved. But be warned, it doesn't mean to say they will stay that way, and it can be an emotional ordeal reaching that point. It's certainly not something you would wish to repeat every evening.

The repercussions of sleep associations become more prevalent as a baby ages and matures, coinciding with advancements in brain development, greater awareness of their surroundings and an ability to perceive change.

It's easy to pigeonhole your child as either a good or bad sleeper. Most often this is not the case at all. In fact, the existence or absence of sleep associations play a vital role in whether a child sleeps well or not. Understanding your toddler's sleep associations, and the impact these have on sleep quality, plays a central role in driving high quality sleep behaviours.

Changing Habits

The upside of all this is that sleep associations can be changed with appropriate application and training. I am not saying it is an enjoyable process. It's not! But you can correct these habits, even if they are the result of years of accidental parenting mistakes.

I can attest that after learning more about sleep associations and their role in my eldest child's behaviour I made significant strides settling my toddler to sleep and keeping her that way. This information was a godsend for me.

In saying that I still wish I had put the appropriate sleep associations in place from when Amber was a small baby... it would have made the next couple of years of my life markedly more manageable.

A review of different sleeping strategies

Over the next few pages I want to touch on a few of the more common sleeping strategies, considering the pros and cons of each. In particular we'll examine the 'No Tears' Method, Crying It Out, Fading and Co-Sleeping.

Now, first of all it's important to clarify I am not advocating for any of these particular strategies over another. There are elements of each that may or may not work for you. No single sleep strategy is effective for every growing baby or toddler.

You will need to formulate your own sleep strategy, taking the in depth understanding you have of your own children, some of the recommendations in this book, and then figure out what works for your situation.

'No Tears' Method

Many parents associate sleep training methods with hour upon hour listening to their baby or toddler cry its little heart out. This can be devastating, and no wonder many parents avoid this confrontation.

But sleep training does not necessarily mean holding firm as your baby wails, providing little or no comfort. The 'No Tears' or 'No Crying' method of sleep training is a gentler approach to teaching your child to sleep. The name 'No Tears' might be a little misleading (tears are inevitable when mixing children and sleep!) however this approach is proposed to ensure fewer tears.

The theory is that parents nurse their child to the point of drowsiness through rocking, feeding or similar, providing comfort and support prior to sleep. The baby or toddler is placed in bed calm but awake to practice the art of falling asleep unassisted. If a baby cries out an immediate response is advocated regardless of the timing. Cuddling or more feeding is common. Often parents stay in the room at the onset of sleep and after wakening to minimise crying. Supporters of this procedure believe it is a better way to develop positive sleep associations than crying induced alternatives.

The pros of No Tears are relatively obvious. Less crying provides an identifiable tick mark, minimising the trauma of baby and parent during the settling process. This method also encourages a strong connection between mother and child.

On the flip side, opposers of this method are critical of the overt dependence on comfort from parents at bedtime - hypothesising it renders it increasingly difficult for children to learn to soothe themselves. Even champions of this method will readily admit it can take longer than other methods to deliver results and that it won't work for every family.

Every sleep training method requires an element of preparatory work - strengthening bedtime routines, modifying feeding habits, instituting environmental changes to make a room more 'sleepy'. This prep work is potentially more critical to the No Tears method in order to achieve results.

'Crying It Out'

Crying it out (CIO) sometimes referred to as Ferberizing following the 1985 book 'Solve your Child's Sleep' by Paediatrician Richard Ferber. Ferber is often acknowledged as one of the driving forces behind the Crying It Out method.

The underlying theory says allowing your baby to cry it out and fall asleep of its own accord will break poor sleep associations. The theory assumes falling asleep is a skill every baby can master and parents simply need to step back and provide them the opportunity to do so.

Ferber was convinced crying is an unavoidable part of sleep training. He suggests it's acceptable for babies to cry for a specific period of time before comforting them. Interestingly, the idea of crying it out has morphed from Ferber's original premise of setting limits on when to respond and offer comfort (reassuring a baby before leaving again) to leaving a child to cry for as long as it takes to get them to sleep.

In Ferber's theory he doesn't ever actually reference 'Crying it Out'. Instead he focuses on increasing the time between comforting on subsequent nights and always exiting the room while the baby is still awake.

Crying It Out has garnered widespread support from other child sleep specialists. Michael Cohen, a paediatrician and author of The New Basics: A to Z Baby & Childcare for the Modern Parent advocates a similar approach believing that babies can be left to cry for as long as necessary from only 8 weeks of age.

The primary benefit of CIO is that many children successfully learn to sooth or self-settle at bedtime or when waking during the evening without constant parental intervention. Parents who have successfully used this method maintain it can be difficult listening to your beloved child screaming, but suggest marked improvements can be noticed within a few days - short term pain for long term gain.

Of course this approach will not work for every child, even when parents are consistent. Drawbacks of this method are firstly that you are going to lose some sleep for a few nights at least. It is inevitable. Secondly, listening to your child in distress and the arduousness of not allowing yourself to intervene can be really challenging.

Opponents believe there are kinder and gentler ways to teach babies to sleep and many are strong believers that babies do better when they are held than when left to cry. It is true that with this method a really determined baby continues to cry for long and stressful periods. CIO is not something that can be used with really young babies; you need to wait until your child is of a suitable age to implement CIO, and even then it isn't guaranteed to work for everyone.

Adult Fading

Adult Fading, also commonly known as 'camping out' is a less well known approach to No Tears and a gentler version of sleep training than Crying It Out. Parents turn to fading when they are looking to avoid the cold turkey approach of CIO, but are not necessarily convinced No Tears will provide enough impetus to change their child's behaviour. Fading effectively falls between the two earlier practices.

What is Fading? It is a sleep training approach where the parent gradually diminishes their role in helping a child get to sleep. Rather than simply leaving them to cry, the parent 'camps out', sitting in a chair in the baby or toddler's room. The theory states that parents minimise the time they 'camp out' each night or move farther way, until suddenly... they're gone! The benefit of fading is that it can be implemented when children are as young as 5 months old, and proponents believe it provides a balance between too little comfort and too much. The method tends to minimise tears associated with CIO, and it can be adapted for toddlers and pre-schoolers if required. The cons or perceived downside of Fading however is that your child is still reliant on the sleep association of a parent or adult in order to drift off to sleep.

Co-Sleeping or Sleep Sharing

Maybe some of you might argue that co-sleeping is not necessarily a strategy for training your child to sleep, instead it is a sleeping environment designed to minimise the incidence of undesirable sleeping behaviours from your baby or toddler.

This may be true, and in reality if you are ever going to reclaim your bed, you'll probably still need to find an alternative approach to sleep training at some stage.

This is not a method that I encourage mainly due to safety reasons. But, with that being said I am still going to touch on the 'strategy' of co-sleeping with your child, as some parents have used it successfully to ensure their child achieves a quality and duration of sleep required to function optimally. One survey suggested 13% of parents are co-sleeping with their offspring.

The theory behind co-sleeping is that babies or toddlers sleep better next to their parents. A physical connection creates a strong bond between (usually) mother and child, and it also has the advantageous upside of minimising the task of getting out of bed throughout the night, simplifying night feeding.

There are a number of cons that do make co-sleeping an unappealing option for many parents. If you toddler is particularly unsettled in bed this can impact the quality of your own sleep. It might be time for a bigger bed to avoid overcrowding. This arrangement can also cause you to wake more readily for fear of rolling on your tiny baby or infant.

I should also mention the impact that welcoming a child into your bed semi-permanently can have a negative impact on the relationship between husband and wife. If co-sleeping is your strategy of choice and you are able to achieve the desired sleep for you and your toddler then it can be a worthwhile option. Although, I would hasten to add that too often sleep sharing is done without due consideration and as a last resort to get baby or toddler to sleep.

Introduction to self-settling

Self-settling is a hot topic. Everyone with babies, infants or toddlers regularly reference a child's ability to self-settle, as do sleep training specialists or academic experts. Why is it so important that you child can fall asleep by his or herself?

As your child ages various changes occur to their sleep cycle. One of these changes can be the tendency to wake between cycles causing several wakings a night. In most cases these disturbances to your toddler's sleep will last but a few seconds or perhaps a minute or two. Don't worry, this behaviour is perfectly normal and shouldn't disturb your child or your sleep appreciably.

That is… so long as they have learned how to self-settle; to drift back off to sleep without your help. If however your child has not mastered the skill of self-soothing and relies heavily on your support, a specific sleep association, or certain routine to sleep, such as feeding or rocking, then it is a different story.

This story ends with your child waking you up several times during the night to complete the onerous process of persuading your child to go back to sleep.

Teaching your child to self-settle is not only advantageous in encouraging high quality rest for your young boy or girl, it will also mean you get a better night's sleep ongoing.

What Works: 10 Steps to Success

We have touched on a few of the common mistakes parents make when trying to put our children to sleep. We've mentioned sleep associations and the integral role they play in a toddler's sleep patterns. We have also briefly reviewed some of the popularised methods for encouraging your child to sleep.

Bedtime Battles: No More!

Now it must be time for me to impart my wisdom ... and reveal what I believe are the key steps to transforming your baby or toddler to a point where they love going to bed and sleep with a sense of calmness and acceptance.

You can't force a child to fall asleep. If only. That would make life a whole lot easier right?! However, you can support your toddler to improve his or her bedtime behaviour and allow them to get to sleep quickly and more easily. It is important to remember that every child is unique. What works for your friend's toddler may not work for yours. What was successful for your first child may require refining for a subsequent baby or babies. There is an element of 'what works for you' in getting your baby or toddler to sleep.

However, in saying that, there are specific things that you need to avoid and components that you need to introduce, regardless of your chosen strategy or outcome, in order to build a better bedtime routine. It also pays to remember that it can take up to six weeks for habits to be changed particularly if these habits have been long embedded in your toddler's behaviour.

So, without further ado let's consider 10 steps to developing successful toddler sleep habits:

1. Encouraging self-settling

We touched on the importance of self-settling or soothing earlier in this chapter. Teaching your child the skill of settling themselves is vital to a good night's rest. Brief waking in the night can occur at any age. It only becomes a problem if the child cannot go back to sleep without intervention from parents.

A study published in the Journal of Sleep Research demonstrated parental interventions encouraging independence and self-soothing were linked to higher total sleep volume at night as well as attaining longer lasting periods of uninterrupted sleep, when compared to more active interactions.

(http://www.ncbi.nlm.nih.gov/pubmed/19021850?dopt=Abstract)

So, how do you encourage your child to self-soothe? There are a number of key steps to teaching your toddler to sleep without your assistance.

• Decide on (and don't falter, stay strong) your approach

The first and possibly most important considerations when teaching your child to self-soothe is determining how you intend to respond when your child is struggling to master the art of self-settling. Are you going to endorse the Crying it Out approach? Is a No Tears strategy, allowing for reassurance to an upset child your preferred option? Or do you want to institute a Fading technique to overcome months of co-sleeping or parental reliance?

The exact approach will depend on your individual situation. Once you have determined your optimal plan of action, it's important to allow sufficient time to create a change in habit. Remember, self-settling is like teaching any skill to your growing child, it will take time and practice. Think how long it takes them to master the skill of crawling or walking.

• Put your child to bed drowsy BUT still awake.

A key to indoctrinating the art of self-setting is putting your child to bed when they are still awake. Ideally, they will be drowsy and ready to sleep, but don't fall into the habit of letting them fall asleep while feeding if you can avoid it. You want your young boy or girl to create a sleep association with their bed or cot. Ideally the bed or cot should be in their own room.

Placing them in bed in a drowsy state will allow them to create the desired link between their bed and sleep and is a key contributor to a toddler's ability to self-settle. If you are continually feeding or comforting a child to sleep and then transferring them this will be their strongest sleep association.

The same rules apply when a toddler requires assistance during the night. While feeding is necessary for a baby depending on their life stage, a healthy toddler shouldn't need food or drink throughout the night. Avoid providing milk or water when they wake, and worst of all giving them juice or other sugary beverages. They don't need a sugar rush at 2am in the morning, or an increased risk of tooth decay. Continued feeding of your child at night can impact their ability to potty train, so there is another good reason to restrict their milk supply.

• Don't indulge grizzling

Avoid the temptation to check on your child when they are grizzling in their bed. As a concerned parent it's a natural urge to want to try to calm or quieten your child when endeavouring to settle them to sleep. You need to fight this urge. Children can take some time to drift off to sleep.

Grizzling is normal and is a sign that your child is tired and in need of rest. He or she might self-settle without your intervention. If the grizzles turn into real crying you may decide to intervene and reassure your toddler, depending on your preferred settling technique, but it is important to allow time for your child to try to settle themselves to sleep.

• Absent yourself

A key to encouraging self-settling is the absence of a parent when your child drifts off to sleep. Try to ensure you have

97

left the room before they take the count, and aspire to get them to sleep in their own bed or sleeping environment.

When your toddler does wake in the evening, take stock before rushing into their bedroom. Try to slow your response down, allow them time to settle on their own terms. Avoid getting into bed with them to encourage sleep.

• Track your progress

One thing I found useful when training my children was tracking progress. Simply using a pen and notebook I began maintaining a record of how quickly they were settling. This allowed us to see if their ability to self-settle was improving (as this can become cloudy in the midst of constant tiredness).

So, when can babies or toddlers begin to self soothe? How long should you wait before beginning to teach your child this skill? You can actually begin this process with your baby from day one.

Sure, they will probably not pick up the skill straight away… it is a bit of a shock to the system to be outside mum's body in the great wide world. However, implementing appropriate tactics early on, such as putting your child to sleep drowsy will support your teaching efforts when your baby is ready to self-settle.

By the time your toddler gets to four or five months of age - ensuring they have acquired the skill of self-soothing is essential if you wish to get a good night's sleep.

2. Create a solid bedtime routine

At what point in time can you implement a consistent bedtime ritual? Some experts believe that from three months onwards you should employ a solid bedtime routine of between 30 and 40 minutes.

A well-devised and regular bedtime routine is a central component of improving sleeping habits. If you observe toddlers that sleep soundly and go to bed with minimal fuss you'll often discover this is driven by a familiar routine in the lead up to bedtime.

A recent study supports the establishment of a consistent bedtime routine. Researchers examined the impact of bedtime routine on infant and toddler sleep, as well as maternal mood. The study reviewed 405 mothers and their children, aged between 7 months and 3 years. Two age-specific three week studies compared existing night-time behaviours with a newly created bedtime routine.

The results demonstrated a significant reduction in problematic sleep behaviours with a consistent bedtime routine. Toddlers were faster to drop off to sleep and exhibited lower incidence of night wakings. Not surprisingly, maternal mood also improved markedly. Everyone loves a sleeping baby!

Bedtime should be a special time for you and your child. It's a wonderful opportunity to interact with your toddler, providing them security and comfort, and furthering an already strong parent / child bond.

How do you go about creating a bedtime routine then? And what exactly are you trying to achieve? I imagine a battle free bedtime is most parents' goal. In order to define your routine you need to delineate between what your child wants at bedtime and what he or she actually needs.

A key constituent of a bedtime routine is that it is consistent and replicable. It needs to be repeated every night to form a habit and set an expectation with your child. It should be designed in a way that will encourage your toddler to wind down and relax. Start by determining how long you want the routine to be. Make sure you establish limits within your routine and remain in charge; however it's also useful to allow your growing child some independence, providing elements of choice or control throughout the process.

What are the essential components of a bedtime routine? This really is up to you. The fundamentals of a bedtime routine should be determined by individual parents. But take care that your ingredients include quiet, calming yet enjoyable activities. Avoid pursuits that excite your young child.

Here are a few ideas you might wish to incorporate into your bedtime routine:

• Bath time

A warm bath after dinner can be a soothing experience that de-stresses and calms your child, easing them into bedtime. Don't let bath time turn into playtime - where every toy under the sun finds its way into the tub and water is sprayed from floor to ceiling. Quiet relaxation and gentle scrubbing should be the focus.

• A bottle or night-time feed

A warm bottle of milk or, depending on your child's stage of maturation, breast feed is a common element of a night-time routine. Topping up your child to allow for prolonged sleep is always recommended. The timing of this feed is however, of utmost importance. Avoid allowing your child to take the bottle to bed or feeding them to sleep. Try to incorporate bottles earlier in your routine to enable your child to fall asleep of their own accord.

• Teeth brushing

Bedtime Battles: No More!

Not only is encouraging your child to brush his or her teeth before bed an important lesson and mandatory for general oral hygiene, toddlers will start to associate the process of teeth cleaning with an impending bedtime.

• Choose your pyjamas

Getting your child into pyjamas probably doesn't feel like part of a well defined routine, rather an obligatory step in getting them into bed. However, changing into warm, comfortable sleepwear, or a new nappy, after a bath signifies another progression towards bed. Allowing your toddler to choose their preferred sleeping attire or PJs provides independence and 'buy in' to the routine.

• Debrief on the day's events

Just before bed is a wonderful time to talk about a toddler's day. What were the three things they enjoyed most today, how did specific activities make them feel, what they are looking forward to (after a sleep) tomorrow. Quiet discussion not only provides your child with attention and comfort, it also gives them a wonderful parent / child activity they can look forward to at the end of the day.

Rather than talking about the day's occurrences, an alternative may be to tell a story about yourself, perhaps focusing on memories from your childhood.

• Read a bedtime story

A nice way for a toddler to slow down and relax in the evening is by reading them a bedtime story. Ask then to choose their favourite book from the bookshelf or from a small selection. No doubt you will get the same book over and over again for days or weeks! Don't worry, this is great for their learning, and again provides them some input into the bedtime ritual.

• Sing a lullaby

Do you have a great singing voice? Even if you don't your child won't complain. A quiet lullaby or song can help advance your toddler into a drowsy state. A quick rendition of ABC or Mary Had A Little Lamb should do the trick.

• Say your goodnights

The final step of your routine should be a quick cuddle, kiss and to say your goodnights, whilst letting your child know you're leaving the room. Now it is time for sleep.

The key thing to remember in this process is the word 'routine'. If you incorporate elements of the practice one night and not the next don't be surprised if you struggle to motivate your child to sleep. Creating a recurring and consistent pattern that your child understands and accepts is integral to its success.

I said it before, but I will mention it again here. Stimulating or high energy activities such as running around, playing outside, screen time and other similar pursuits should be avoided. Consumption of foods or drinks with sugar or caffeine such as chocolate and fizzy drinks should also be prohibited. It's really important to set clear boundaries around what is and isn't acceptable as you transition towards bedtime. Make sure your toddler is aware of the restrictions.

3. Construct a suitable sleep environment

How often do you go into your child's room and find toys piled up around them after they have eventually drifted off to sleep? As you slowly try to extract every Matchbox car, My Little Pony or Transformer, sure enough you manage to wake them from their slumber.

Setting the stage for sleep is critical to encouraging long lasting uninterrupted sleep. Remember the sleep association discussion we had earlier? You want to manufacture a setting in your child's room that is conducive to good sleep. So, what is the perfect sleep environment?

• Calm and relaxing

First and foremost the sleep area needs to be calm and relaxing and should be easily identified as their sleep zone. You want to establish positive sleep associations that are sustainable.

• The right temperature

Not too hot, not too cold. The temperature in your child's sleeping area is critical. You don't want your baby shivering when the temperature bottoms out before dawn. You also want to avoid warming the environment to a level that makes them sweaty and uncomfortable.

Some experts believe slightly cooler temperatures allow children to sleep more effectively. Regardless, the key consideration is that extremes in either direction make sleeping more difficult. The temperature should allow toddlers to remain warm with light covers, avoiding bulky bedding that will be thrown off or become tangled.

• Free from distractions

It's tempting to decorate your young child's room with a lavish amount of toys and books. There is no arguing it makes the room look inviting and exciting for a young child. However, as soon as your toddler progresses to a big bed these distractions can become a barrier to sleep. Ideally your room should minimise distractions such as toys that are readily available. Otherwise your child will inevitably spend a good portion of the evening traipsing throughout his or her room and playing with their favourite toys.

• Appropriate lighting

What is appropriate lighting? It's critical that your child's room emphasises the difference between night and day so lighting should be dim or dark, encouraging the release of sleep encouraging melatonin. A nightlight is often useful so the child still recognises the sleeping environment as well as to avoid the child becoming fearful of pitch black conditions. Eliminate the use of overhead lights, especially when you check on them at night.

• Keep it quiet

Minimising noise is important as your toddler moves into the transitional sleep stage. At this point the slightest noise can stir your baby. Once they have progressed into deep sleep they're less likely to wake so you don't need to tip toe around all evening.

In saying this, it's still favourable to diminish significant household noises where possible such as leaving for work or arriving home, especially if you park right outside a toddler's window.

• Sleep props

We talked about sleep props and their addictive nature. The key point here is if you make the conscious decision to administer some form of sleep prop (such as a snuggly toy or dummy); make sure it is readily available throughout the entire evening. If it becomes displaced ensure your young child knows how to find or reapply it.

4. Set bedtime

"What time do I need to go to bed?" Ideally the answer is "the same time as every night". Selecting an appropriate bedtime is really important. The time shouldn't be about what is convenient for you as a parent, it's what is appropriate for your child. I mentioned the role bedtime plays in setting a child's internal clock earlier remember?

How do you go about selecting the right bedtime? Well, the first objective is that you and your toddler should try to go to bed and wake up at the same time every day.

• Start with the sleep guidelines

Yes, we discussed that national guidelines are not appropriate for every child but they're still a worthwhile starting point. Familiarise yourself with age appropriate guidelines from sleep experts. Now, based on your child's general waking hour, work out when they may need to go to bed.

• Consider your child's behaviour

Do you find your toddler's behaviour deteriorating hours before bedtime? When you attempt to put them to bed are they unmanageable? Hyperactive? Does it seem like they are not ready for sleep? While some will mistake this extra energy as a sign a child is not ready for bed, it may actually mean their current bedtime is too late in the evening.

• Difficulty getting to sleep

Nowadays there is a tendency for kids to go to bed later and obtain less sleep than they need. Is it always really difficult to get your child to sleep? If you are nodding your head it could mean your child is going to bed too late. On the flip side, if you are following a strong bedtime routine but your toddler just doesn't seem ready to drift off, or plays in their cot for a significant amount of time - you may have your bedtime on the early side. It may take a little trial and error to determine the optimal timing for your child.

• Wake up time

Wake up time is also an important consideration. This can be impacted by the time your child goes to bed, so it pays to consider this in your calculations. Remember, we discussed earlier that moving your bedtime later doesn't necessarily mean a sleep-in come morning?

If your child is waking too early don't simply opt for a later bedtime as a knee jerk reaction. It is feasible they may need to go to bed earlier to ensure longer and better quality sleep.

My kids have always maintained a reasonably consistent morning wake up time. I have however, had to intervene at times during longer naps to minimise interference with nightly sleep. Make sure you also set predictable and consistent nap routines.

Once you've established your child's bedtime, make sure you stick to it. If you believe your toddler is going to bed too late at present, it might be time to shift him or her to a more suitable hour. The best approach may be a gradual movement over a few days or weeks. That way you (may) avoid significant resistance.

Changing your child's bedtime can be a fiery battleground. Toddlers love to test boundaries. How do you overcome a stubborn toddler hell bent on staying up?

A couple of useful strategies that worked for me were - firstly trying to anticipate the needs of my children, and secondly - providing them with some control over how they went to bed.

This might sound like a scary proposition, but it certainly helped when encouraging them to trot off to bed.

What do I mean by anticipating needs? Think of the excuses your toddler comes out with during their bedtime routine. Do they always ask for water, a trip to the toilet, or complain of being cold? Take care of these issues before bedtime to remove the likelihood of raising them as an objection during the settling process.

By letting your child have a say in their bedtime routine I certainly don't mean they get to rule the roost. They still follow your routine and you set and enforce the rules. However, you might give them small elements of control along the way such as what water bottle they would like their water in, their choice of bedtime story, or similar.

5. Reassure... don't comfort

Now, I imagine my view here may be controversial. When our first child was a baby I would resort to comforting frequently in order to get her to sleep. I didn't realise I was creating reliance on parental love and comfort every time she stirred. If you are consistently feeding your child to sleep, rocking or cuddling your baby while he or she drifts off to sleep, this is probably a primary contributor to your baby's inability to doze off without your help.

I now understand reassurance is preferable to soothing a child with affection. I am not opposed to entering my child's room, I mentioned earlier that crying it out didn't work for us at all, but on entry I prefer to focus on behaviours that reassure her she is safe and loved, and that it is time for sleep. This allows my child to discover their own way of going to sleep rather than relying on me.

There is sometimes confusion between what's meant by reassurance versus comforting. Let's consider some examples of what reassurance is…

• Quiet affirmation to put your child's mind at rest

• Verbally assuring your child

• Providing minimal calming action

• Speaking in a firm voice to advise it is "time for sleep"

• Intermittently returning to calm or dispel a child's fears

• Leaving promptly when a child calms down

• Quickly re-adjusting bedding / tucking in

Reassurance is not:

• Picking up your child

• Cuddling your child to provide support or encourage sleep

• Patting or stroking to assist sleep

• Staying with your child until he / she is asleep

• Remaining in close proximity (unless adopting the Fading technique)

• Taking your child out of the bedroom

• Lying beside your child's cot

It is true that some children struggle with certain sleep training techniques and seek parental comfort. Particularly those who suffer from separation anxiety or are extremely temperamental. While you may find you need to adjust your designated approach to settling your child along the way, regardless of the technique I still recommended you avoid excessive cuddling or comforting to get your child to sleep.

6. Ignore complaints and protests

Toddlers often don't go down without a fight. I (now) like to think it shows a bit of character. The key is to avoid becoming involved in a power struggle with your toddler! You might not always win.

Stay calm, be firm and advise your child it is bedtime... and then continue your dedicated bedtime routine. If somewhat inevitably, your toddler continues to push the boundaries arguing and bellowing their point - swiftly provide a consequence. It may be leaving the bedroom until the abuse stops!

The following four step process is a useful one when facing a barrage of complaints or protests.

• Ignore

If you ignore a complaint, often a child's short attention span will render the accusation short lived.

• Explain

If not... and your toddler continues their line of questioning, the next port of call should be to briefly explain the 'why' to your child. For example: "Why can't I stay up as late as my brother?" Fairness often means sameness in a child's language! It might be stating that "two and a half year olds need more sleep to grow than five year olds". Then, calmly reassure them it is bedtime and time to go to sleep.

• Withdrawal

Following explanation, avoid getting into a long winded debate. Leave the room and withdraw from the discussion.

• Consequence

If the initial three steps have failed to resolve an issue and your child either won't stay in bed or protests more vocally it may be time to provide a warning. Speak calmly and briefly and leave. Don't get drawn into an argument. If the behaviour continues - swiftly follow up with the consequence promised. Perhaps it is shutting the door for a predefined period of time.

If your toddler continues to push the boundaries - reapply the consequence or perhaps increase the length of time the consequence is delivered for. Don't forget to inform your child they are in control of whether or not the consequent continues to occur. And even during this combative period - make sure you maintain your normal sleep environment and atmosphere - keep it dark and quiet. Stick to your routine.

Hopefully your efforts to calm your child are successful. When they do calm down or listen, make sure you acknowledge their good effort with praise. "I'm proud of you for calming down".

7. Leave the room

You have completed your pre-established bedtime routine. Bubs is in bed but still awake. What's next? Leave the room. Gently remove yourself from the equation to let your baby or toddler get started on the all-important task of putting themselves to sleep.

Why leaving the room is important.

Hopefully the answer to this is reasonably obvious after reading the rest of my book, but for the sake of clarity, staying in your toddler's room creates a sleep crutch or negative sleep association.

It is not simply important to leave. You need to be somewhere your child cannot hear you. If he or she is aware you are nearby they will feel they are missing out... and the crying is sure to ensue.

Sometimes, when you leave your child will become upset. This is inevitable and normal. Timed 'check ins' can be a worthwhile response. Enter the room and verbally reassure your child at predefined intervals, then leave again. Aim to increase the period of time between 'check ins' over the period of a few days.

Admittedly, if your child has developed a habit of sleeping in your bed, or you have indulged her or him by lying beside them, it might not be reasonable to all of a sudden demand a child stays in their bed the entire night or goes cold turkey on parental involvement. In this case you may wish to make separation a more gradual process such as outlined in the Fading technique.

Fading allows for a parents presence, 'camping out' in a child's room. Make sure you continue to put your child to bed drowsy and avoid comforting - the act of Fading is designed to simply reassure a child with your presence. While I'm not necessarily a strong advocate of this approach, I do recognise in some cases, such as after a long period of co-sleeping, it may be a suitable alternative.

If you do decide to adopt this method, rather than leaving the room immediately when your child goes down, you might place a chair near their bed and 'camp out' until they fall asleep. Over the period of a couple of weeks you should gradually increase the distance from chair to bed until voila - you can simply leave the room after wishing your child goodnight.

8. Familiarity

If you were to ask me the most important ingredient in convincing your toddler to adopt a high quality sleep structure ... I'd probably start by telling you they are all important! Pressed, I would say that familiarity and routine were the cornerstones of our ability to turnaround our unenviable toddler sleeping habits and create a sleeping environment in our house that is significantly more agreeable.

According to Jodi Mindell, associate director of the Sleep Centre at Children's Hospital of Philadelphia, familiarity is really important. She stated "each additional night that a family is able to institute a bedtime routine, and the younger that the routine is started, the better their child is likely to sleep."

Ensuring our girls were familiar with our planned routine, understood our new rules or approach, and knew what to expect was central to our remarkable turnaround. Once embedded it reduced arguments, became accepted and most importantly of all - meant that myself, my husband and my girls achieved high quality sleep as a result.

How do you ensure you child is familiar with a new sleep routine?

• Educate

Sit down with your child and explain to them the fantastic new routine that they are going to start at night times. Make them aware of every step of the process so they know what to look forward to.

• Excite

Dress your new routine up as an exciting new approach. What a great way to get ready for bed! It might pay to make the last part the most exciting for your toddler. Perhaps it is a bedtime story, a quiet song or whatever their favourite component of the process is.

• Visual

To help your child understand the new process a chart or image might increase familiarity. Demonstrate the process in pictures so they can refer and keep track. Even implementing a start chart style approach could be useful - let them tick off that the bedtime routine is completed every night.

9. Be persistent and consistent

Change is not easy, particularly when dealing with babies or toddlers. We are all aware young children often lack self-control and require structure to be set for them. The key to all of the steps above is being persistent and consistent in your approach.

Yes, you will need to prepare for some hard work along the way. It's not easy dragging yourself out of bed at 2am, bleary eyed, attending to an upset daughter and walking her back to her room. It's difficult stopping yourself caving in under special circumstances, when your child is ill, or distressed due to a recent nightmare. However, you can still reassure your child without inviting her into your bed.

Teaching your toddler the consequences of coming out of their room is important, whether it is a briefly closed door or otherwise, and rewarding them for a great sleep with positive language and encouragement is beneficial.

Most important is making sure mum and dad are on the same page. Make sure you both buy in to the process and stick to predefined rules and consequences. Don't let dad come home five minutes before bed and get the kids super excited and hyped up. Five minutes of fun could give you a night-time of pain.

Make sure both of you are consistent with your sleep training plans and share the workload. I know sometimes this is difficult... particularly if a toddler only wants a certain parent's attention. But this is where parents need to dictate terms. Take joint responsibility in getting your child to sleep.

As you undertake the often rigorous process of teaching your child to sleep, be firm and calm. Don't give up, and stick to your plan. You should see improvements in a few weeks (maybe less!).

10. Introducing a sleep clock

One of the elements I found particularly useful as a part of our revamped bedtime routine, and I believe played an important role in regulating both of my daughters' sleep patterns, was the introduction of a sleep clock.

I did some research and found that there were a bunch of these sleeping aids available, and armed with my newly acquired knowledge of sleep associations I thought I would include one in my daughter's sleeping environment.

I imagine you're familiar with the concept of a sleep clock? However, for the sake of clarity, the idea of a sleep clock is that it teaches timings for waking and sleeping to a young child, providing a reference point plus a tool to encourage them to go back to sleep as well as when they are allowed to get out of bed in the morning.

Now I know what you are thinking. Toddlers can't tell the time! Yes, agreed. Children don't know what time it is, and when they wake at 4am they might be mistaken to believe it is morning. A sleep training clock provides a simple visual change from night-time to demonstrate morning and when your toddler is allowed to get out of bed.

While it's easy to argue wake up times with mum and dad, in theory the clock is objective and cannot be argued with.

My girls enjoyed the process of putting the clock 'to sleep' and I firmly believe it reinforced the message about staying in bed and asleep at night time. The integration of a sleep training clock alongside the other structural changes to our approach I have outlined played a vital role in reclaiming control of our evenings.

Chapter 6: Sleepy Starz Sleep Clock

Ok, we've briefly discussed the supporting role a sleep training clock played in overcoming my eldest daughters sleep issues. The training clock was also instrumental in ensuring we didn't suffer a repeat dose of sleep deprivation with daughter number two. I can't overstate how useful we found sleep clocks as a teaching tool for our toddlers, both encouraging sleep behaviours and providing a sense of independence for them during the sleep process.

While a lot of the sleep clocks on the market are useful and possess similar features, my husband and I did recognise a number of features we thought would have been beneficial for our individual situation, and presumably for parents leveraging clocks for a similar purpose.

Because of the benefit we derived from these sleep training devices, and the opportunities we observed to take sleep training to the next level, my husband and I embarked on the grand scheme of creating our own: The Sleepy Starz Clock!

Developing this has been a labour of love, and despite my oldest child now having grown out of a reliance on her clocks (she can tell the time herself now!) we are really excited about assisting other families struggling with their toddler's sleep training. Our Sleepy Starz Sleep Clock has been in
117

development for the past 24 months and we are delighted about the release of our product to the market.

What makes Sleepy Starz different from other sleep training clocks?

Somewhat consistent with other sleep clocks, the aim of the Sleepy Starz Sleep Clock is to teach children when to go to sleep, when to stay in bed and when they are allowed to get out of bed.

Typically, young children are unable to grasp the concept of time, so the Sleepy Starz Sleep Clock demonstrates to children night-time and daytime with a series of relevant, fun, yet calming images that children can relate to. Parents input the time they want their child to wake, and there are seven scenes parents and toddlers can choose from depending on their preference. Images are displayed on the screen throughout the night, and at the defined wake up time, a day version of the image will appear. This signals to the child it is time to get up.

Seven different scenes and three sleep settings allow for variability between children. For example, the moon crossover setting has a series of night images in which a moon slowly crosses over the sky. The child can see that it's close to morning time when the position of the moon is on the far right hand side of the screen. The star countdown setting has a series of night images where stars slowly fade from the screen throughout the night.

A big part of our guiding philosophy when developing this product was an understanding that each child is different and there is not a single correct approach to teaching sleep principles to children. Our clock provides parents and toddlers with a range of choices and features to choose to suit each individual.

Other features the Sleepy Starz Sleep Clock possesses include:

• A brightness controller which allows the sleep clock to be used as a night light

• A 15 minute countdown feature where the day image of a chosen scene appears on the screen for 15 minutes before fading away to night-time images. This allows parents to prepare children for bed

• An optional lock feature so the clock settings cannot be changed by the child

• A picture story book to add further depth to the night-time routine

• A free teddy bear in the packaging. The teddy bear, called 'Sleep Tight Ted' features within the Sleep Clock

We are really very proud of the Sleepy Starz Sleep Clock and are hopeful that it provides many parents throughout Australia and the world with an improved night's sleep moving forward!

If you would like to find out further information on Sleep Starz Sleep Clock please visit sleepystarz.com. Feel free to also contact me through the website - http://www.sleepystarz.com/contact_us.php for any information/advice relating to your child's sleeping habits/issues.

Chapter 7: Summary

Thank you for reading my book. I hope you have found it an insightful and useful resource to help improve your infant or toddler's sleeping habits. As a mother who has 'been there' I really appreciate what you are going through balancing the needs of your toddler or family with a personal lack of sleep. It can be a heartbreaking experience at times and I totally empathise with your situation.

One of the purposes of this book was to demonstrate to suffering parents there is light at the end of the tunnel. You can overcome your sleep-deprived nightmare. The magnitude of change we cultivated after implementing a more programmatic and scientific approach was astounding. We managed to completely turn our toddler's sleeping issues around, developing her into a really effective sleeper.

Replicating the processes that had worked on our first child and executing them early with number two meant we avoided a relapse. Even during times when she was unwell or teething she maintained her effective routines.

The purpose of mentioning this is not to rub salt into your wounds or to boast that we are now getting the sleep we require in our household. Hopefully, this provides you with encouragement and hope. No matter how hard the sleep hurdle seems, you can turn things around.

I mentioned this earlier in the book, but it really wasn't until I recovered from chronic sleep deprivation that I truly understood the emotional, mental and physical toll it was having on me. The impact of sleep loss on my child was easier to diagnose. Her lack of concentration, low energy and behavioural impacts were far reaching.

I implore you to take time to analyse or audit your child's (and your) sleep performance. Compare the results to the general guidelines and ascertain how much more sleep your child may need. Remember, a child may require more or less than the guidelines state. Behaviour issues or recurring illness should provide an indicator of sleep debt.

Not only is getting to sleep at an appropriate hour important, equally critical is sleeping well. You and your child need to achieve a mix of deep restorative sleep, to rejuvenate brain and body, and REM sleep so that learning and creativity can thrive.

We discussed that sleep issues are mostly behavioural or environmental and can be alleviated through planning, structure and persistence. However, if you are concerned your sleep issues could be more serious don't be afraid to seek medical advice. A few hours in a doctor's waiting room is worth it to eliminate weeks or months of worry.

Ok. Now is the time to take a step back, try to put any excuses to one side and identify mistakes you may have been making. Try to recognise sleep associations or props your child is reliant on and finally to start to compile a strategy to get on top of your sleep issues.

Make sure you and your spouse or partner work together as an effective team. If one parent is tired or waning, the other needs to step in to the lion's den. Mothers, you don't need to do it all on your own.

Bedtime Battles: No More!

Finally, if you make a concerted effort to follow our ten steps to success I am confident a sleeping baby or toddler will be the end result. Regardless of your chosen strategy, whether Crying It Out, or minimising tears through another approach, the 10 steps still hold true. Work your way through them and modify them to fit your unique situation.

Just remember, it won't happen overnight... but with a bit of resilience and consistency... it will happen.

www.ingramcontent.com/pod-product-compliance
Lightning Source LLC
LaVergne TN
LVHW091152080426
835509LV00006B/653